Ancient-Modern Worship

Ancient-Modern Worship

A PRACTICAL GUIDE TO BLENDING WORSHIP STYLES

Martin Thielen

ABINGDON PRESS
Nashville

ANCIENT-MODERN WORSHIP
A PRACTICAL GUIDE TO BLENDING WORSHIP STYLES

Copyright © 2000 by Martin Thielen

Library of Congress Cataloging-in-Publication Data

Thielen, Martin, 1956–
    Ancient-modern worship: a practical guide to blending worship styles/Martin Thielen.
        p.   cm.
    Includes bibliographical references.
    ISNBN 0-687-03103-6 (alk. paper)
    1. Public worship.   I. Title.

BV15.T445   2000
264—dc21   99-057365

All Scripture quotations, unless otherwise noted, are taken from the New Revised Standard Version of the Bible. Copyright © 1989 by the Division of Christian Education of the National Council of the Churches of Christ in the United States of America. Used by permission.

Those noted TEV are from Today's English Version—Old Testament: Copyright © American Bible Society 1976; New Testament: Copyright © American Bible Society 1966, 1971, 1976, 1992. Used by permission.

Those noted KJV are from the King James Version of the Bible.

In chapter 3, the tale about the baker is based on a story told by Syd Lieberman at the 1991 National Storytelling Festival in Jonesborough, Tennessee. Lieberman adapted the story from Rabbi Zalman Schachter's *Gates to the City*. Copyright © 1983 Avon Books, New York.

The "John Todd" drama sketch in chapter 3 is based on a story told by Dr. John Claypool in his sermon, "Working Through Grief," 28 May 1978, at the Northminster Baptist Church in Jackson, Mississippi.

In chapter 7, the story about the church custodian is based on a Carlyle Marney story retold in Roger Lovette's *Come to Worship*. Copyright © 1990 Broadman Press.

Publishers and copyright owners have given permission to use quotations from the following copyrighted works:

Eucharist: Christ's Feast with the Church, by Laurence Hull Stookey. Copyright © 1993 Abingdon Press. Used by permission.

00 01 02 03 04 05 06 07 08 09—10 9 8 7 6 5 4 3 2 1

MANUFACTURED IN THE UNITED STATES OF AMERICA

For

Paula,

Jonathan,

and

Laura

Preface

⚭

Journal Entry: Sunday afternoon, August 1994.

Last night I visited a Saturday evening contemporary worship service at Community Fellowship Church. I liked the vibrant music; the use of media and visual arts; the strong sense of community; and the effort to be relevant to contemporary culture. However, the service lacked a sense of transcendence, flow, and congregational responsiveness, and was far more human-centered than God-centered.

This morning I visited Christ Cathedral Church. I liked the pageantry of the processional, the ancient architecture, the historic liturgy, the atmosphere of transcendence, and the centrality of the Eucharist. The service, however, lacked warmth. The focus was almost all head and no heart, the atmosphere seemed stiff and rigid, and the music failed to speak to my heart.

In spite of their many strengths, both of these worship experiences were inadequate for me. What I long for is worship that includes both ancient and modern expressions of praising our Creator. I want the warmth, creativity, and celebrative atmosphere of modern worship. However, I also want the sacramental, liturgical, and transcendent dimensions of ancient worship. I suppose I am searching for a kind of "ancient-modern" worship. I believe this style of blended worship is possible, and that it holds tremendous promise for the twenty-first century. With God's help, I hope to create this kind of worship experience for me and for my congregation in the months and years ahead.

Contents

Introduction

A former student, familiar with my passion for worship, once referred to me as a "worship junkie." Although I am not sure I like that term, it is a fairly accurate description. I have written four books, two book chapters, and fifty articles on the subject of worship. In addition, I have served as an editor and consultant in the field of worship, led over one hundred workshops on the topic of worship, and worked as an adjunct professor of worship. As a pastor, I have spent fifteen years planning and leading worship, and even spent a yearlong sabbatical studying worship at Vanderbilt University.

I have spent the past twenty years trying to learn something about the worship of God. In this book I will share some of what I have discovered. Although I would enjoy exploring such important issues as the priority, theology, and history of worship, *Ancient-Modern Worship* focuses on a subject every minister must deal with every week—preparing for Sunday worship. More specifically, it offers practical guidelines for preparing blended worship—worship that incorporates historic, traditional, and contemporary worship styles.

My advocacy of blended worship represents the culmination of a long pilgrimage as a worship leader. My worship journey has taken me through five distinctive phases over the past two decades. A brief overview of that journey follows.

Phase 1: Traditional worship. Upon graduation from seminary, I was called to a medium-sized Baptist church in Arkansas. Having had virtually no worship training in seminary, I quickly adopted a "traditional" pattern of worship. In that denomination, traditional worship meant an opening hymn, a prayer, announcements, another hymn or two, an offering, special music, a fairly lengthy sermon, an invitation, and a closing prayer. It did not take too many years for me to grow tired of this style of traditional worship.

Phase 2: Creative worship. During this phase, I spent a lot of energy attempting to do something new in every service. I created a new worship outline for every worship service and constantly attempted to be novel and different. Unfortunately, the pressure to be "creative" took away the joy from worship leadership. It also diminished the substance and content of our worship services. As a result of these factors, I finally grew weary of this model.

Phase 3: Contemporary worship. The third phase of my worship journey can be called "contemporary" worship. After visiting several high-profile contemporary churches, I decided to adopt a contemporary worship style. I implemented praise choruses, drama, the use of banners, need-based topical sermons, listening guides for sermons, and a host of other innovations. However, after a short period of time I grew disappointed with this style of worship. I felt it lacked transcendence, it tended to be nonparticipatory, and it focused too much on self-actualization and not enough on God. As a result, my journey down this path was fairly short-lived.

Phase 4: Historic worship. I discovered historic worship during a yearlong sabbatical of liturgical studies at Vanderbilt University, and through my experience at a liturgical church in Nashville, Tennessee. In many ways my journey toward historic worship was like coming home. I was deeply moved by the God-centered, transcendent, and sacramental dimensions of this ancient tradition. I was also attracted to its beauty, order, content, and depth. And the sacramental theology I adopted while studying liturgy and worshiping at a liturgical church has profoundly affected my spiritual life, enhanced my experience of God in worship, and transformed my identity as a worship leader. I cannot overestimate how much I owe to the historic tradition of worship. However, as much as I loved (and continue to love) this tradition, something seemed to be missing. The liturgical church I attended was more rigid and formal than I wanted. I missed the spontaneity of my former worship experiences. I missed singing contemporary songs that touched the heart and not just the head. I also missed the warm sense of community and the celebrative atmosphere of contemporary worship. Although I knew that historic worship had much to offer, I also knew that I wanted more.

Phase 5: Blended worship. I have now moved to a fifth, and I believe, final phase of my worship journey—what I call "ancient-modern" worship. In this tradition I have the glorious privilege of taking the best elements of traditional, creative, contemporary, and historic worship, and blending them together in an ancient-modern worship experience. I believe ancient-modern worship is the best of all possible liturgical options, and I wholeheartedly advocate it to other worship leaders.

Chapter 1

An Introduction to Blended Worship

This book provides worship leaders with practical guidance for planning blended worship services—worship that incorporates historic, traditional, and contemporary worship styles. I like to call this blending of old and new worship patterns ancient-modern worship. This style of worship is, in my opinion, the best liturgical option for most Protestant churches in America.

In his book *Blended Worship: Achieving Substance and Relevance in Worship*, Robert Webber claims that people are increasingly interested in historic worship, and that people are also increasingly interested in contemporary worship. Those who are interested in historic worship like its rich tradition, heritage, beauty, order, content, and substance, while people who are interested in contemporary worship like its freedom, spontaneity, joy, warmth, and sense of community. Webber claims that a convergence of these two traditions is occurring, giving birth to a new style of worship that is rooted in Scripture, aware of the developments in history, and passionate about contemporary relevance. Webber calls this convergence "blended" worship, and he believes it represents the future of Christian worship. In his article on convergence worship in *The Complete Library of Christian Worship* (vol. 3, pp. 122-124), Webber lists several characteristics of blended worship.

General characteristics of blended worship include

◇ a willingness to reopen all the questions about worship

◇ a willingness to learn from the entire worshiping community

◇ a healthy respect for the past

◇ a commitment to contemporary relevance

Specific characteristics of blended worship include

◇ a commitment to the ecumenical consensus of the fourfold approach to worship: acts of entrance, the service of the Word, the service of the Table, and the acts of dismissal

◇ a commitment to the celebrative character of worship

◇ a broad range of musical content and styles

◇ a recovery of the arts

As we enter the twenty-first century, blended worship has become more prevalent among U.S. churches. Of course not all churches will, or should, participate in blended worship. There will always be a need for pure liturgical, traditional, contemporary, and charismatic churches. However, it is likely that a large percentage of churches will adopt at least some form of blended worship.

Benefits of Blended Worship

One of the many benefits of blended worship is that it offers an alternative to "worship wars," which pit those who prefer traditional worship against those who prefer contemporary worship. Blended worship also avoids splitting congregations into separate traditional and contemporary worship services, what one church musician calls "carving up the body of Christ." Instead, blended worship allows traditionalists to experience new and fresh expressions of contemporary worship, and offers contemporary enthusiasts an opportunity to experience elements of worship that have nurtured the people of God for centuries. As a result, blended worship can be a "win-win" situation that greatly enhances the worship experience of all persons, regardless of their primary worship preferences.

Several years ago I led a worship conference for pastors in Minnesota and Wisconsin. During the conference, I encouraged participants to take a worship survey of their congregations in order to discover the needs, wants, and preferences of their people. About a month later, one of the pastors who attended the conference called me to say, "I took a worship survey, like you suggested, and discovered that about half of my congregation wants traditional worship, and the other half wants contemporary worship." I replied that instead of presenting a problem, the situation indicated an overwhelming mandate for blended worship.

Over the next three months this pastor and his congregation grappled with this issue. Four possible options were proposed: (1) continue their current style of traditional worship; (2) move to a contemporary style of worship; (3) provide two different worship services, one contemporary and one traditional; or (4) create a blended worship style that incorporated both traditional and contemporary elements of worship. After several church-wide discussions, the congregation agreed upon the fourth option: *blended worship*. About nine months later, the pastor called to say that the blended approach was working extremely well, and that the church had significantly grown since the changes had been implemented.

An important note to remember is that churches sometimes blend old and new worship styles differently. Some churches will follow a predominantly traditional pattern of worship and use only a small percentage of contemporary

17

elements. For example, many liturgical churches retain their historic liturgy and continue to sing traditional hymns. However, they add contemporary elements of worship such as praise choruses and drama sketches. Other churches opt for worship that is predominately contemporary in style. However, they often add various aspects of ancient worship such as the use of historic creeds and more frequent observance of Eucharist. Still other churches divide their services fairly evenly between historic and contemporary elements of worship. Each church must blend the old and new in ways that are appropriate for its particular context.

Some worship leaders claim that blended worship does not work, that in the end it simply frustrates everyone. However, most Christians are willing to accommodate the worship needs of fellow believers, as long as their own worship needs are also taken seriously. Like a family, a congregation can learn to give and take in order to meet the needs of all its members. As time progresses, traditionalists usually come to appreciate and enjoy contemporary elements of worship, and those who prefer contemporary worship come to appreciate and enjoy more traditional aspects of worship. The end result is an enhanced worship experience for all.

Although blended worship is not appropriate for every church, many, if not most churches, could benefit from this approach. I have successfully implemented blended worship in several congregations, including a five-year-old suburban church, a fifty-year-old downtown church, and a one-hundred-year-old small-town church. All three congregations experienced significant growth after introducing blended worship. Do not tell these congregations—and thousands of others like them—that blended worship does not work, because it works for them every Sunday.

Although blended worship incorporates a variety of worship traditions, it is not merely a hodgepodge of old and new worship styles. To be effective, blended worship must follow a dependable, yet flexible, pattern of movement.

A Pattern for Blended Worship

Although this book advocates a specific pattern of worship, no *one* right way to worship exists. Throughout the centuries, the church has worshiped God in many diverse ways. For example, many evangelical churches practice what liturgical scholars call the "frontier model" of worship. Frontier worship developed during the evangelistic camp meetings of the early 1800s in the American West. The basic pattern for frontier worship orders worship services into three basic parts:

◇ a time of praise and prayer, with great emphasis on music
◇ a sermon, usually evangelistic in nature
◇ a public invitation challenging people to respond to the gospel

While there is nothing particularly wrong with this worship pattern, it differs significantly from the eighteen hundred years of biblical and historical worship that preceded it.

A basic order of worship emerged early on in the life of the church; it is called the *biblical-historical pattern* of worship. This pattern has endured centuries of Christian history and is still used in most Christian communities. Early Christian worship emerged from two primary roots: the synagogue worship of ancient Judaism, and the Lord's Supper experience of the Upper Room. The early church fused together what happened in the synagogue (songs, prayer, Scripture, sermon) and what happened in the Upper Room (the Lord's Supper). Therefore, from its earliest days, the church practiced a two-part order of worship:

◇ the service of the Word
◇ the service of the Table

Both of these expressions of worship are found in the New

19

Testament. Acts 2:42 records, "They devoted themselves to the apostles' teaching . . ." (the service of the Word) "[and] to the breaking of bread . . ." (the service of the Table). In addition, Acts 20:7-11 mentions a Sunday worship pattern of Word and Table. We also see images of Word and Table in Luke's account of the Emmaus story (Luke 24:13-35).

This basic pattern of Word and Table was firmly established by the second century. For example, in his *First Apology*, written around 150 A.D., Justin Martyr describes services of Word and Table as the normative experience of Christian worship. Later, the church added to this basic order of worship a gathering and a dismissal, thus providing a fourfold order of worship:

◇ the gathering
◇ the service of the Word
◇ the service of the Table
◇ the dismissal

However, the service of the Word clearly had two parts: the Word itself (Scripture readings and sermon) and a response (affirmation of faith, prayer, and offering). Therefore, in practicality, the basic worship pattern involved five movements:

◇ gathering
◇ service of the Word
◇ response
◇ service of the Table
◇ dismissal

Guided Freedom

This fivefold order of worship has been the mainstay of Christian worship for most of its history. It also serves as the foundation of blended worship. This long-standing pattern offers worship leaders the wonderful gift of guided freedom. The ancient fivefold pattern serves as our basic guide for planning and leading worship. However, within each of the five movements we are free to incorporate historic, traditional, and contemporary expressions of worship. The end result is worship that takes seriously our biblical and historical heritage but also allows full usage of historic, traditional, and contemporary styles of worship.

If we put this ancient pattern of worship together and translate it into a modern worship outline, it looks something like this:

We Gather to Worship God
We Listen to the Word of God
We Respond to the Call of God
We Celebrate at the Table of God
We Depart to Serve God

Notice the six strengths of this worship pattern:

1. It is true to the biblical and historical foundations of worship.
2. It provides a holistic and balanced worship experience.
3. It moves and flows; it provides meaningful progression.
4. It is focused on God.
5. It is highly participatory; the congregation is actively engaged.
6. It is flexible; diversity and creativity can be implemented within each movement.

Chapters 2 through 6 provide practical nuts-and-bolts guidance for planning these five movements of worship. Chapter 7 provides, in story form, a real-life example of this fivefold model of blended worship. The appendixes 1 and 2 include orders of worship based on this model, along with a listing of numerous worship resources. My hope is that this book proves a helpful tool for you as you prepare blended worship services for your congregation.

Let the worship begin!

Chapter 2

We Gather to Worship God

∽

The opening movement of worship is usually referred to as the entrance, acts of entrance, or the gathering. In this movement the people of God gather together for the worship of God. Since we gather to adore God and to celebrate the risen Christ in our midst through the presence of the Spirit, the tone of the gathering is generally festive. The focus is on God—Father, Son, and Holy Spirit—and lifts up the transcendence, majesty, mystery, and holiness of the Almighty.

In the early years of Christian worship, the gathering was quite simple. For example, the worship leader might say, "The Lord be with you." The congregation would respond, "And also with you." Various acts of praise and worship would follow.

During the fourth through the sixth centuries, the gathering expanded. Worship services often began with a processional. While singing, the ministers and other worship leaders, dressed in full vestments, processed in. They carried objects such as a cross, candles, incense, and a Bible. The procession evoked an exciting sense of expectation. A greeting followed. On Easter Sunday, for example, the worship leader might say, "The Lord is risen!" The congregation would respond, "The Lord has risen indeed!" An opening prayer, later called a *collect*, followed. Then the congregation engaged in various acts of praise as an acknowledgment of God's glory. By the fourth century, the church sang the hymn

"Gloria in Excelsis" (also known as the Greater Doxology) at the beginning of many worship services. One version of this ancient hymn goes this way:

> Glory to God in the highest, and peace to God's people on earth.
> Lord God, heavenly King, almighty God and Father, we worship you, we give you thanks, we praise you for your glory.
> Lord Jesus Christ, only Son of the Father, Lord God, Lamb of God, you take away the sin of the world: have mercy on us; you are seated at the right hand of the Father: receive our prayer.
> For you alone are the Holy One, you alone are the Lord, you alone are the Most High, Jesus Christ, with the Holy Spirit, in the glory of God the Father. Amen.
> *(Book of Common Prayer*, p. 356)

A Liturgical Gathering

Liturgical churches still follow this ancient pattern. For example, in the Episcopal church the gathering usually consists of these elements:

◇ silence (usually followed by an instrumental prelude)

◇ an opening hymn (often a processional hymn)

◇ a greeting (Except for the seasons of Lent and Easter, the celebrant says, "Blessed be God: Father, Son, and Holy Spirit." The congregation responds, "And blessed be his kingdom, now and for ever.")

◇ a brief prayer (led by the celebrant, who says, "Almighty God, to you all hearts are open, all desires known, and from you no secrets are hid: Cleanse the thoughts of our hearts by the inspiration of your Holy Spirit, that we may perfectly love you, and worthily magnify your holy Name; through Christ our Lord. Amen" [*Book of Common Prayer*, p. 355].)

24

◇ an act of praise (often the hymn "Gloria in Excelsis")
◇ a collect, or opening prayer (An assigned collect for each Sunday of the year is printed in the *Book of Common Prayer*. The celebrant begins the collect by saying, "The Lord be with you." The congregation responds, "And also with you." Then the celebrant says, "Let us pray." At the conclusion of the collect, the people all say "Amen." At that point the gathering is over and the service of the Word begins.)

A Contemporary Gathering

Contemporary churches follow a very different pattern for the gathering. Recently I visited a contemporary church in Tennessee in which the gathering began with informal singing of praise choruses. At the appointed time of worship, the minister, dressed in casual clothes, welcomed the congregation with, "Good morning and welcome to Fellowship Church. We're glad you're here, and hope this proves to be a meaningful experience of worship for you." Next, the congregation stood and sang a long block of contemporary praise choruses, which were led by a praise team consisting of four singers and a band that had a drummer, two guitarists, a bass player, and a keyboard player. The lyrics were projected on an overhead screen. After about fifteen minutes of singing, the gathering ended with a prayer by the senior pastor, and the service of the Word began. Some contemporary churches offer "seeker services," which have little or no congregational participation. Their gathering usually introduces the theme of the day, often through a video/slide presentation or a musical production that might include both Christian and secular music.

A Traditional Gathering

In traditional Protestant churches, the gathering usually includes the following six segments:

◇ informal greetings, conversation, and fellowship by the congregation before the service begins
◇ an organ or piano prelude
◇ a call to worship—often a responsive reading based on a psalm
◇ an opening hymn of praise, such as "Holy, Holy, Holy"
◇ an opening prayer, usually referred to as the invocation
◇ additional hymns and prayers (A prayer of confession and an assurance of pardon is often included in the gathering.)

A Blended Gathering

The gathering in a blended worship service uses historic, traditional, and contemporary elements of worship. Usually before the service begins, the congregation informally greets and converses with one another. A few minutes before the worship service, the worship leader extends a welcome from the pulpit and calls attention to pertinent announcements. Then, with a statement such as "Let us now take a moment to prepare for the worship of God," the congregation is invited to worship. After a moment of silence, the choir might sing the contemporary chorus "Sing Hallelujah (to the Lord)." The congregation then stands for the call to worship. The worship leader says, "Blessed be God: Father, Son, and Holy Spirit." The congregation responds, "And blessed be God's kingdom, now and forever." The worship leader continues, "Lord, open our lips," and the congregation follows with, "And our mouths shall proclaim your praise." As the organist plays a traditional hymn such as "O for a Thousand Tongues to Sing," the crossbearer, acolyte, banner carrier, choir, and minister process in. At the conclusion of the hymn, the congregation is asked to join in reading the opening prayer, which is printed in the bulletin. The lay worship leader then leads the congregation in a responsive reading of a psalm. After the reading, the congregation sings praise choruses such as "In My Life, Lord, Be Glorified" and "Glorify Thy Name."

A careful examination of this gathering will reveal a blending of historic, traditional, and contemporary elements of worship. Historic elements include the ancient pattern of processing into the sanctuary, the use of vestments and a cross-bearer, and the call to worship: "Blessed be God: Father, Son, and Holy Spirit, and blessed be God's kingdom, now and for ever." Traditional elements include the opening hymn, "O for a Thousand Tongues to Sing," and the opening printed prayer. Contemporary elements include the singing of praise choruses and the use of banners. Although three different traditions are used in this gathering, they flow and fit together extremely well.

The remainder of this chapter will offer suggestions for planning blended gatherings. The following elements will be reviewed:

- ◇ pre-service activities
- ◇ announcements
- ◇ preparation for worship
- ◇ call to worship
- ◇ processional or opening song
- ◇ opening prayer
- ◇ other acts of praise
- ◇ resources for congregational singing

Pre-Service Activities

Before the worship service formally begins, while the people are gathering, one or more of the following options may take place:

- ◇ *Informal conversations, fellowship, and greetings.* This time of greeting reminds worshipers that they come to worship not only as individuals but also as part of a community of faith.

- ◇ *Instrumental music.* Live or taped instrumental music can be played before the service begins. Since the opening movement of worship is primarily celebrative in nature, festive music selections should be highlighted.
- ◇ *Informal singing of hymns and choruses.* Many contemporary and blended churches sing songs for ten to fifteen minutes before the service formally begins. Choruses such as "Praise the Name of Jesus" and hymns such as "Brethren We Have Met to Worship" are often used during this time. Members of the congregation are sometimes invited to choose the songs they want to sing.
- ◇ *Rehearsal of an unfamiliar song that will be sung during the upcoming worship service.* As a result, when the congregation sings the new song, they will be familiar with the tune, and singing will be enhanced.
- ◇ *A time of silent meditation.* Unless this is part of your tradition, as it is in many liturgical churches, it is unlikely to happen without intentional effort on the part of the worship leaders. However, if a time of silence is desired before the service begins, it can easily be done. Have a worship leader stand at the front of the church and greet the congregation saying, for example, "In the book of Habbakuk we read, 'The LORD is in his holy temple; let all the earth keep silence before him' (2:20). At this time let us observe a moment of silence as we prepare for the worship of God." Instrumental music can be played during this time of meditation.

Announcements

Unfortunately, church announcements during worship services are probably here to stay, since Sunday morning worship is the largest gathering of the congregation during the week. An important issue concerning announcements is where to place them. There is no ideal place. Probably the best place to make announcements is immediately prior to the service. Placing the announcements at this point in the service emphasizes the important issues in the life of the church without interfering with the flow of worship. The announcements can be concluded with, "Let us now prepare for the worship of God."

Preparation for Worship

After the announcements, the congregation needs an opportunity to prepare for worship. Many possibilities exist for this important moment of worship. Consider these ten options.

1. *An instrumental prelude.* A traditional prelude is still an effective method to prepare a congregation for the worship of God. Although the prelude is customarily organ or piano music, consider using other instruments as well, such as a guitar, flute, violin, or trumpet. A handbell choir is another good alternative. Almost any instrument or combination of instruments can be used during the prelude.

2. *Gathering songs.* As noted earlier, gathering songs have replaced the prelude in many contemporary churches, and serve as an effective preparation for worship. Churches that hold more formal services sometimes sing gathering songs and also include a prelude before worship begins.

3. *Choral music.* Traditionally called the introit, this brief opening song by the choir (or ensemble group) is an effective way to prepare for worship. In churches that process to the altar, the introit is sung from the back and/or sides of the sanctuary.

4. *A slide presentation.* For example, nature scenes can be projected onto an overhead screen while a soloist sings or an instrument plays a familiar song of praise, such as "How Great Thou Art."

5. *A video clip.* Many contemporary churches use video

clips in their worship services. For example, a worship service might begin with a short video clip from the movie *The Shawshank Redemption*, showing the scene where an elderly man is released from prison after serving fifty years. As he walks the streets of the city, he feels overwhelmed by all the hustle and bustle. During this scene he recites a letter to his friends in prison, saying, "The world has gotten itself into a great big hurry." After the video clip, the pastor or worship leader could say to the congregation, "We live in a noisy and busy world that seldom gives us time to think, reflect, or pray. However, in the Bible, God tells us that we need times to 'Be still and know that I am God' (Ps. 46:10). As we begin our service today, let's do exactly that: Let's be still and know that God is God." Afterward, a prelude, perhaps played on a guitar or saxophone, could begin.

6. *A solo*. An appropriate solo can serve as an effective preparation for worship. For example, "In This Very Room" can be used to prepare the congregation for a Communion service. Or begin Easter worship with "Was It a Morning Like This?" One church began its service with a unique solo of "Brethren We Have Met to Worship." The soloist began the song while seated in the congregation. She sang the first stanza a cappella as she slowly walked to the altar, and was joined by the instrumentalists on the second and third verses. Then the entire congregation stood and sang along with her on the fourth verse.

7. *A Scripture reading and solo combination*. I began one Good Friday service by reading selected verses from Isaiah 53 concerning the suffering servant. During the reading the pianist softly played the hymn "O Sacred Head, Now Wounded." Then immediately following the reading a soloist sang that hymn.

8. *Drama*. Although drama is usually performed during the service of the Word, short drama sketches can also be used as preparation for worship. For example, an Easter Sunday service could begin with women in biblical costumes walking down the aisle of the sanctuary. As they walk, they talk to one another about the death of Christ. Offstage a

voice proclaims, "Do not be afraid; I know that you are looking for Jesus who was crucified. He is not here; for he has been raised, as he said. Come, see the place where he lay. Then go quickly and tell his disciples, 'He has been raised from the dead . . .'" (Matt. 28:5-7). As the women joyfully run offstage, the choir sings "He Is Alive" from the old musical *Celebrate Life.* The song begins, "*He* is alive, he is *alive*, he *is* alive. . . ." Afterward, the worship leader could lead a brief call to worship by saying, "Christ is risen!" The congregation could respond, "Christ is risen indeed!" Follow with the processional hymn "Christ the Lord Is Risen Today."

9. *Liturgical movement or dance.* A growing number of churches are using movement and dance in their worship services. When I was pastor of a church in Hawaii, we often used Christian hula as a part of our gathering. In that setting, dance was a natural and beautiful expression of praise. While it is unlikely the gathering at most churches will include the hula, liturgical dance can add much to the experience of worship. Liturgical movement can be a highly effective way to begin a worship service. Consider using the following movement, accompanied by a soloist or choir singing the first stanza of "O Come, O Come, Emmanuel," at the beginning of an Advent service.

O come, O come,
[*On knees, head bowed, knuckles of hands on the floor on each side of the body, fingers pointing backward. Drag hand forward slowly, bringing hands up, palms still down.*]

Emmanuel,
[*Bring arms up high with palms up, face uplifted*]

And ransom captive Israel,
[*Right arm moves downward behind body. Left arm moves down and back. Wrists are together, so hands appear like tied hands of prisoner.*]

That mourns in lonely exile here
[*Head bows to floor*]

31

Until the Son of God appear.
[*Head comes up slowly. Arms come to front and move up slightly, with palms up.*]

Rejoice! [*Bring torso and arms up quickly, right knee is on the floor, place left foot on the floor*]

Rejoice! [*Stand! Throw arms up!*]

Emmanuel [*Arms lower, extend out in horizontal position*]

Shall come to thee,
[*Bring arms in, hands 8" apart, palms up*]

O Israel. [*Arms sweep back, head and torso bow slightly, right foot steps backward*]

(*Worship Through the Seasons: Ideas for Celebration*, p. 6)

10. *Poetry and other readings.* Occasionally begin a worship service with a poem or reading. For example, plan a worship service that focuses on environmental stewardship. Begin the service with this adaptation of St. Francis of Assisi's "Canticle of All Creation":

Reader 1:   Most High, all powerful, all good Lord! All praise is yours, all glory, all honor, and all blessings. To you alone, Most High, do they belong. No mortal lips are worthy to pronounce your name.

Reader 2:   All praise be yours, my Lord, through all that you have made, and first my Lord Brother Sun, who brings the day and light you give us through him. How beautiful is he, how radiant in all his splendor! Of you, Most High, he bears the likeness.

Reader 1:   All praise be yours, my Lord, through Sister Moon and Stars; in the heavens you have made them bright and precious and fair.

Reader 2:   All praise be yours, my Lord, through Brother Wind and Air, and fair and stormy, all the weather's moods, by which you cherish all that you have made.

Reader 1: All praise be yours, my Lord, through Brother Fire, through whom you brighten up the night. How beautiful he is . . . Full of power and strength.

Reader 2: All praise be yours, my Lord, through Sister Earth, our Mother, who feeds us in her sovereignty and produces various fruits with colored flowers and herbs.

Readers 1 and 2: All praise be yours, my Lord!

Reader 1: Through Brother Sun and Sister Moon,

Reader 2: Through Brother Wind, and Sister Water,

Reader 1: Through Brother Fire and Sister Earth,

Readers 1 and 2: All praise be yours!

After the reading, the congregation can stand for the call to worship by the worship leader: "Lord, open our lips." The congregation may respond, "And our mouths shall proclaim thy praise." A processional hymn such as "All Creatures of Our God and King" may follow.

Also consider using choral readings. A youth group could perform the following choral reading from Psalm 100 (KJV).

Males and Females: Make a joyful noise unto the Lord, all ye lands.

Males: Serve the LORD with gladness:

Females: Come before his presence with singing.

Males: Know ye that the LORD he is God:

Females: It is he that has made us, and not we ourselves,

Males and Females: We are his people, and the sheep of his pasture.

Males: Enter into his gates with thanksgiving,

Females:	And into his courts with praise:
Males:	Be thankful unto him,
Females:	And bless his name.
Males and Females:	For the LORD is good; his mercy is everlasting; And his truth endureth to all generations.

Call to Worship

The call to worship comes immediately after the preparation for worship, and prior to the opening song.

(Note: Churches that use a processional sometimes place the call to worship after they process in. This allows the minister to enter with the choir and other worship leaders and then lead the call to worship.)

Occasionally the preparation for worship also serves as the call to worship, and the congregation can move immediately into the opening song. The previous choral reading of Psalm 100 is a good example. In that case, a separate call to worship would be unnecessary. However, in most cases, a formal call to worship, sometimes called the greeting, is advisable. It should be brief, and doxological in nature. These calls to worship are usually a responsive act between leader and people. A variety of examples follow.

Leader:	Blessed be God: Father, Son, and Holy Spirit,
People:	**And blessed be God's kingdom, now and forever. Amen.**
Leader:	LORD, open our lips,
People:	**and our mouths will declare your praise.**
	(Ps. 51:15 adapted)
Leader:	I was glad when they said to me,
People:	**"Let us go to the house of the LORD!"**
	(Ps. 122:1)
Leader:	This is the day that the LORD has made;
People:	**let us rejoice and be glad in it.**
	(Ps. 118:24)

34

Leader: The grace of the Lord Jesus Christ be with you.

People: **And also with you.**

Leader: The risen Christ is with us.

People: **Praise the Lord!**
                                (*The United Methodist Hymnal*, p. 6)

Leader: Praise the LORD! Praise, O servants of the LORD; praise the name of the LORD.

People: **Blessed be the name of the LORD from this time on and forevermore.**

Leader: From the rising of the sun to its setting the name of the LORD is to be praised.

People: **The LORD is high above all nations, and his glory above the heavens.**

Leader: Praise the LORD! Praise, O servants of the LORD;

People: **Praise the name of the LORD.**

Leader: The Lord be with you.

People: **And also with you.**

Leader: Who are you?

People: **We are the people of God.**

Leader: Who made you?

People: **God our Creator made us.**

Leader: Where do you live?

People: **We live in God's good world.**

Leader: Why are you here?

People: **We are here to worship God.**

Leader: Then let the worship begin!
              (adapted from *Writing Your Own Worship Materials*, p. 23)

Leader: Ascribe to the LORD, O families of the peoples,

People: **ascribe to the LORD glory and strength.**

Leader: Ascribe to the LORD the glory due his name;

People: **bring an offering, and come into his courts.**
                                                (Ps. 96:7-8)

Leader: Worthy is the Lamb that was slain

People: **to receive power,**

Leader: and riches,

People: **and wisdom,**

Leader: and strength,

People: **and honour,**

Leader: and glory,

People: **and blessing.**

Leader: Worthy is the Lamb that was slain.

(Rev. 5:12 KJV)

Leader: This is the day that the LORD has made; let us rejoice and be glad in it.

People: **Like Miriam, let us sing with gladness, for our God triumphs over evil and oppression.**

Leader: Like Hannah, let us pray with grateful hearts, for the LORD our God hears our prayer.

People: **Like Jacob, let us wrestle with God, for out of such struggles new faith is born.**

Leader: Like Abraham, let us respond to God's calling, for in faith's journey we find our lives.

People: **This is the day that the LORD has made; let us rejoice and be glad in it.**

(Be Thou Present: Prayer, Litanies, and Hymns
for Christian Worship, p. 6)

Leader: Sing to the LORD, all the earth!

People: **Tell of God's salvation from day to day.**

Leader: Declare God's glory among the nations,

People: **God's marvelous works among all the peoples!**

Leader: For great is the LORD, and greatly to be praised.

People: **Sing to the LORD, all the earth!**

(1 Chr. 16:23-25 adapted)

Leader: Glory to you, LORD God of our fathers;

People: **you are worthy of praise; glory to you.**

Leader: Glory to you for the radiance of your holy Name;

People: **we will praise you and highly exalt you for ever.**

Leader: Glory to you in the splendor of your temple;

People: **on the throne of your majesty, glory to you.**

Leader: Glory to you, seated between the Cherubim;

People: **we will praise you and highly exalt you for ever.**

Leader: Glory to you, beholding the depths;

People: **in the high vault of heaven, glory to you.**

Leader: Glory to you, Father, Son, and Holy Spirit;

People: **we will praise you and highly exalt you for ever.**
(Book of Common Prayer, p. 90)

Leader: You are worthy, our LORD and God,

People: **to receive glory and honor and power,**

Leader: for you created all things,

People: **and by your will they existed and were created.**
(Rev. 4:11)

Leader: May Jesus' promise, "Where two or three are gathered in my name, there am I in the midst of them," be fulfilled in us.

People: **Make us a joyful company of your people, so that with the faithful in every place and time, we may praise and honor you, God Most High. Amen.**
(Book of Worship: United Church of Christ, p. 60)

Leader: I will bless the LORD at all times;

People: **his praise shall continually be in my mouth.**

Leader: O magnify the LORD with me,

People: **and let us exalt his name together.**
(Ps. 34:1, 3)

A variation of this approach is to do a three-part call to worship using the choir, the leader, and the congregation.

Although this works well, sometimes brief instructions are needed to avoid confusion.

Leader:	This is the day that the LORD has made;
People:	**We will rejoice and be glad in it.**
Choir:	*Enter into his gates with thanksgiving, and into his courts with praise;*
People:	**Be thankful unto him, and bless his name.**
Leader:	For the LORD is good; his mercy is everlasting.
All:	**Come, let us worship the LORD.**

Other variations are also available, such as splitting the reading among the leader, the people on the right side of the sanctuary, and those on the left side. In addition, the reading might be divided between the leader, the men, and the women. The following three-way call to worship could be used for a Communion Sunday:

A:	Come, let us celebrate the supper of the Lord.
B:	**Let us make a huge loaf of bread and let us bring abundant wine as at the wedding feast of Cana.**
A:	Let the women not forget the salt,
B:	**Let the men bring the yeast.**
All:	Let the guests come, the lame, the blind, the crippled, the poor.
A:	Come quickly. Let us follow the recipe of the LORD.
B:	**All of us, let us knead the dough together with our hands.**
All:	Let us see with joy how the bread grows.
A:	Because today we celebrate the meeting with the LORD.
B:	**Today we renew our commitment to God.**

(*Thankful Praise: A Resource for Christian Worship*, pp. 30-31)

When preparing the call to worship, be mindful of the season of the year. For Advent one of the following could be used:

Leader:	A voice cries out: "In the wilderness prepare the way of the LORD,

People: make straight in the desert a highway for our God."

(Isa. 40:3)

Leader: Praise be to God!

People: Blessed be the LORD God of Israel, who has visited and redeemed the people.

Leader: Blessed is he who comes in the name of the LORD.

People: Blessed be the name of the LORD.

Leader: Now is the time of watching and waiting.

People: The time of pregnant expectation of new life.

Leader: Now is the season of hope unfolding,

People: the dark winter season when hope is waiting to be born.

Leader: Let us come before God with receptive and willing spirits.

People: May our souls magnify God's name, and may our spirits rejoice in God our Savior!

All: Rejoice! God comes to bring the birthday of life and hope. Amen.

(Bread for the Journey: Resources for Worship, p. 19)

These calls to worship are appropriate for the season of Lent:

Leader: Bless the LORD who forgives all our sins.

People: His mercy endures for ever.

Leader: Come now, and let us reason together, saith the LORD: though your sins be as scarlet,

People: they shall be as white as snow;

Leader: though they be red like crimson, they shall be as wool.

(Isa. 1:18 KJV)

Leader: Come, let us walk in the light of the LORD,

People: that he may teach us his ways, and that we may walk in his paths.

(Isa. 2:5 adapted)

39

For the Easter season one of the following could be used:

Leader	Alleluia! Christ is risen!
People:	The LORD is risen indeed! Alleluia!

Leader:	O sing to God a new song.
People:	**For God has done marvelous things.**
Leader:	Because of God's steadfast love to Israel,
People:	**All the ends of the earth have seen the victory of our God.**
Leader:	For now is Christ risen from the dead!
People:	**Make a joyful noise unto God, all the earth.**
Leader:	Break forth into joyous song and praises.
People:	**For God will rule the earth with righteousness. Nothing in all creation can separate us from the love of God in Jesus our risen Christ. Amen.**

(Bread for the Journey: Resources for Worship, p. 43)

Additional seasonal calls to worship for Advent, Christmas, Lent, Easter, and Pentecost can be found in denominational books of worship (see appendix 2). See also *Bread for the Journey: Resources for Worship* and the *New Handbook of the Christian Year.*

Processional or Opening Song

The opening song follows the call to worship and is often accompanied by a procession of the worship leaders. The opening song helps worshipers to focus on the praise of God, and should be a vibrant, familiar song of adoration to the Almighty. A traditional hymn or a contemporary praise chorus would be appropriate.

Examples of opening hymns:

- ◇ "All Creatures of Our God and King"
- ◇ "All Hail the Power of Jesus' Name"
- ◇ "Come, Christians, Join to Sing"
- ◇ "Come, Thou Long-Expected Jesus"

◇ "Come, Ye Thankful People, Come"
◇ "Crown Him with Many Crowns"
◇ "Holy, Holy, Holy"
◇ "Immortal, Invisible, God Only Wise"
◇ "Joy to the World"
◇ "Joyful, Joyful, We Adore Thee"
◇ "Lift High the Cross"
◇ "Morning Has Broken"
◇ "O for a Thousand Tongues to Sing"
◇ "O Worship the King"
◇ "Praise to the Lord, the Almighty"

Examples of opening choruses:

◇ "We Will Glorify"
◇ "How Majestic Is Your Name"
◇ "We Have Come into His House"
◇ "Majesty, Worship His Majesty"
◇ "All Hail, King Jesus"
◇ "Great Is the Lord"
◇ "Be Exalted, O God"
◇ "Lord, I Lift Your Name on High"
◇ "Enter into His Gates"
◇ "We Bring a Sacrifice of Praise"
◇ "Hymn of Glory"
◇ "This Is the Day"
◇ "Hail to the King"
◇ "We Bow Down"
◇ "Let There Be Glory, Honor, and Praises"

Although the opening song does not have to be accompanied by a processional, the processional adds much to the service. This ancient ritual adds a dynamic and joyous atmosphere of coming before the Lord for worship, and makes a profound impact on the vitality of the worship service. If your church does not process regularly, consider doing so at special times of the year, such as Advent, Christmas, Pentecost, and Easter.

Guidelines for the Processional

◇ All participants in the processional should assemble at the rear of the church before the preparation for worship begins.

◇ The order of the processional should be the cross-bearer; the acolyte(s), or candlebearer(s) if candles are used; the banner carrier(s); a Scripture reader, who may carry a Bible; the choir; and the minister(s).

◇ The processional begins as soon as the opening song starts. The congregation, now standing, joins the worship leaders in singing the processional song.

Opening Prayer

After the opening song comes the opening prayer, sometimes called the invocation, gathering prayer, or collect. This brief prayer acknowledges God's presence with the worshiping community. A simple example of an opening prayer is, "Almighty God, we know you are in this place today. Give us eyes to see you and ears to hear you, through Christ our Lord. Amen."

Some churches precede the opening prayer with the traditional salutation to prayer:

Leader: The Lord be with you.
People: **And also with you.**
Leader: Let us pray.

Several examples of opening prayers follow:

An ancient opening prayer: Almighty God, to you all hearts are open, all desires known, and from you no secrets are hid: Cleanse the thoughts of our hearts by the inspiration of your Holy Spirit, that we may perfectly love you, and worthily magnify your holy name; through Christ our Lord. Amen. (*The Gregorian Sacramentary*, seventh century; as adapted in the *Book of Common Prayer*, p. 355)

A traditional opening prayer: O God, you are infinite, eternal and unchangeable, glorious in holiness, full of love and compassion, abundant in grace and truth. Your works everywhere praise you, and your glory is revealed in Jesus Christ our Savior. Therefore we praise you, blessed and holy Trinity, one God, forever and ever. Amen.

(*Book of Common Worship*, p. 51)

A contemporary opening prayer: Eternal God, help us to worship you today. Give us voices to sing your praise. Give us minds to understand your Word. Give us courage to respond to your call. Help us in this hour to love you with all of our heart, mind, soul, and strength, and to love our neighbor as ourselves. We pray in the name of Jesus Christ our Lord, who taught us to pray together, saying, "Our Father, who art in heaven . . ." Amen.

Further examples of opening prayers can be found in denominational books of worship (see appendix 2). The *Book of Common Prayer* includes an opening prayer (in both traditional and contemporary language) for every Sunday of the year. It is a tremendous resource for preparing the opening prayer of the gathering. Another helpful resource is *And Also with You: Worship Resources Based on the Revised Common Lectionary, A, B, and C.*

It should be noted that many churches add a prayer of confession and an assurance of pardon during the gathering. These prayers are more appropriate during the third movement of worship—"We Respond to the Call of God" (see chapter 4).

Other Acts of Worship

Although it is possible to conclude the gathering with the opening prayer and move directly to the service of the Word, other acts of worship can also be added. Any authentic expressions of adoration and praise are appropriate. For example, many contemporary churches sing an extended block of congregational hymns and/or praise choruses during this time. Some churches have a time of congregational greeting—or "passing of the peace"—during the gathering, often between the opening song and the opening prayer. Although it is appropriate to include the passing of the peace in the gathering, it has historically been placed between the service of the Word and the service of the Table (see chapter 4). Other possible acts of worship during the gathering include

- ◇ Scripture readings (especially from Psalms)
- ◇ responsive readings
- ◇ hymns
- ◇ choruses
- ◇ solos
- ◇ choral music
- ◇ instrumental music
- ◇ drama
- ◇ media presentations
- ◇ intentional silence
- ◇ liturgical dance
- ◇ poetry
- ◇ handbells

During the gathering, I sometimes prepare a literal "ancient-modern" experience of worship for the congregation. We begin by reading, either in unison or responsively, an ancient text of praise and follow it with one or more modern songs. The ancient text might be biblical, such as Psalm 95, 96, or 150; or Revelation 4:8-11 or 5:11-14; or one of the songs of adoration in the opening chapters of Luke: the Song of Mary (1:46-55), the Song of Zechariah (1:68-79), or the Song of Simeon (2:29-32). On other occasions we read in unison an ancient but nonbiblical text of praise, such as "Gloria in Excelsis" or "Te Deum Laudamus," which is a hymn from the fourth-century church. The words of this ancient hymn, presented in a responsive-reading format:

Leader: We praise you, O God.

People: **We acclaim you as Lord; all creation worships you, Father everlasting.**

Leader: To you all angels, all the powers of heaven, cherubim and seraphim, sing in endless praise:

People: **Holy, holy, holy Lord, God of power and might, heaven and earth are full of your glory.**

Leader: The glorious company of the apostles praise you.

People: **The noble fellowship of prophets praise you.**

Leader: The white-robed army of martyrs praise you.

People: **Throughout the world the holy church acclaims you: Father, of majesty unbounded, your glorious, true and only Son, and the Holy Spirit, advocate and guide.**

Leader: You, Christ, are the King of glory, the eternal Son of the Father. When you became incarnate to set us free, you humbly accepted the Virgin's womb.

People: **You overcame the sting of death, and opened the kingdom of heaven to all believers.**

Leader: You are seated at God's right hand in glory. We believe that you will come to be our judge.

People: **Come then, Lord, and help your people, bought with the price of your own blood, and bring us with your saints to glory everlasting.**

(*The United Methodist Hymnal*, no. 80)

Other examples of ancient worship texts can be found in the *Book of Common Prayer*. After reading one of these biblical or historic texts, consider singing a contemporary chorus or a traditional hymn, or one of each.

Resources for Congregational Singing

Since congregational singing is such a vital part of worship, especially during the gathering, it is important to have several sources of appropriate material. The kind of music used during the gathering or any other movement of worship will depend, to a large degree, on the particular context. Some churches will choose primarily traditional music, while others will choose contemporary music. Blending both old and new music styles is desirable, since both play an important role in the worship of God. The praise choruses help us express love and praise toward God in new, emotive, and meaningful ways. Older hymns connect us to a long and important heritage, and help root us in important theological truths. Although the blend need not be fifty-fifty, some blending of old and new is the best musical option for most churches.

Traditional hymns and songs can be found in denominational hymnbooks, while collections of contemporary songs are available from numerous music publishing houses. See appendix 2 for further information.

Chapter 3

We Listen to the Word of God

O nce the gathering is over, the people of God are prepared to listen to the Word of God. Regardless of worship style, the primary two elements in the service of the Word are the reading of Scripture, and the sermon. However, other forms of proclamation are also appropriate; they include drama; liturgical movement; media presentations; poetry and other readings; testimonies; banners and other forms of visual art; and various kinds of music.

The Priority of Scripture

The reading and interpretation of Scripture have been essential components of Christian worship since biblical times. In the eighth chapter of Nehemiah, Ezra read Scripture to the people of God with profound results. Luke 4:16-22 records that Jesus went to the synagogue, read from the Scriptures, and discussed the reading with the people. Paul told Timothy in 1 Timothy 4:13, "Until I arrive, give attention to the public reading of scripture . . . ."

By the third century, the service of the Word included readings from the Law, Prophets, Epistles, book of Acts, and Gospels. Psalms were sung between the readings. Responses to the reading of God's Word were eventually developed. For example, the reader would say, "A reading from the book of the prophet Isaiah." Then the reader would read the text. Immediately following the reading the person would say, "The word of God." The congregation would respond, "Thanks be to God."

Additional pageantry developed around the reading of the Gospel lesson. When it came time in the service to read the Gospel, worship leaders processed to the center of the congregation. They carried the Bible, along with candles and incense. Then the reader said, "The gospel of our Lord Jesus Christ as recorded in John (or Luke, Mark or Matthew)." The now standing congregation responded, "Glory to Thee, O Lord." After the reading, the worship leader raised the Bible over his head and said, "The gospel of our Lord." The congregation responded by saying, "Praise to Thee, O Christ." This tradition continues today in some liturgical churches.

Many churches each week follow a lectionary of Scripture readings from which the sermon is based. Readings may include an Old Testament, Epistle, and Gospel reading, and a psalm. Over the course of three years of lectionary readings, all major biblical passages are covered. A listing of lectionary readings can be found in any denominational book of worship. Regardless of whether a church follows the lectionary, the reading and exposition of Scripture should be a significant part of every worship service.

Enhancing Scripture Readings

For the public reading of Scripture in worship, consider the following suggestions for enhancing biblical readings within blended worship services.

1. *Pray before the reading.* Many churches offer a prayer, often called the "Prayer for Illumination," before reading the Scripture lessons. Examples of this prayer are as follows:

> Lord, open our hearts and minds by the power of your Holy Spirit that, as the Scriptures are read and your Word proclaimed, we may hear with joy what you say to us today.

Gracious God, we do not live by bread alone, but by every word that comes from your mouth. Make us hungry for this heavenly food, that it may nourish us today in the ways of eternal life, through Jesus Christ, the bread of heaven. Amen.

(*Book of Common Worship*, p. 90)

Additional prayers of illumination can be found in the *Book of Common Worship* on page 60 and on pages 90-91.

2. *Sing before the reading*. Songs of illumination, both traditional and contemporary, can be sung immediately prior to the reading of Scripture. They include

- ◇ "Break Thou the Bread of Life"
- ◇ "Blessed Jesus, at Thy Word"
- ◇ "Wonderful Words of Life"
- ◇ "Spirit of the Living God"
- ◇ "O Word of God Incarnate"
- ◇ "Open My Eyes, That I May See"
- ◇ "Thy Word Is a Lamp"
- ◇ "Alleluia"
- ◇ "Thy Word"
- ◇ "Open Our Eyes, Lord"
- ◇ "Holy Spirit, Mighty God"

See *Renew! Songs and Hymns for Blended Worship* for other suggestions.

3. *Add a response before the reading*. The reader might say, "This is the word of the Lord, let us have ears to hear." In many liturgical churches, the reading is preceded by the words, "A reading from _____" (the citation is given). Prior to the Gospel reading, the reader says, "The Holy Gospel of our Lord Jesus Christ according to _____." The people respond, "Glory to you, Lord Christ."

In a liturgy from Zaire, the following exchange between the worship leader and the congregation occurs before the reading of the Gospel lesson:

Leader:	Brothers and sisters: The Word was made flesh,
People:	**And he dwelled among us.**
Leader:	Let us listen to him.

(Baptism and Eucharist: Ecumenical Convergence in Celebration, p. 206)

4. *Add a response after the reading.* Here are two examples:

Leader:	This is the word of God for the people of God.
People:	**Thanks be to God.**

Leader:	Those who have eyes to see,
People:	**let them see!**
Leader:	Those who have ears to hear,
People:	**let them hear!**

(adapted from the Gospels)

5. *Print the passage in the bulletin and read it in unison.*
6. *If the text is set to music, sing it.* Over thirty-five examples of Scripture songs can be found in *Renew! Songs and Hymns for Blended Worship* (see appendix 2).
7. *Create a litany using the text.* Almost any biblical passage can be rewritten into a responsive-reading format. For example:

Leader:	Love is patient; love is kind;
People:	**love is not envious or boastful or arrogant or rude.**
Leader:	It does not insist on its own way;
People:	**it is not irritable or resentful;**
Leader:	it does not rejoice in wrongdoing,
People:	**but rejoices in the truth.**
Leader:	It bears all things,
People:	**believes all things,**
Leader:	hopes all things,
People:	**endures all things.**
All:	**Love never ends.**

(1 Cor. 13:4-8*a*)

Leader:	O come, let us sing to the LORD;
People:	**let us make a joyful noise to the rock of our salvation!**

Leader:	Let us come into his presence with thanksgiving;
People:	**let us make a joyful noise to him with songs of praise!**
Leader:	For the LORD is a great God,
People:	**and a great King above all gods.**
Leader:	In his hand are the depths of the earth;
People:	**the heights of the mountains are his also.**
Leader:	The sea is his, for he made it,
People:	**and the dry land, which his hands have formed.**
Leader:	O come, let us worship and bow down,
People:	**let us kneel before the LORD, our Maker!**
Leader:	For he is our God,
People:	**and we are the people of his pasture, and the sheep of his hand.**

(Ps. 95:1-7)

As discussed in chapter 2, the text can be divided into a three-way reading between leader, choir, and congregation. Or, the reading can be divided between the left and right sides of the sanctuary, or between the men and women.

8. *Present a dialogue Scripture reading.* If there is dialogue in a text, consider having several people take on the various roles. A narrator will need to read all the nondialogue passages. Here is an example from the passion narrative in the Gospel of John.

Narrator:	Then Pilate took Jesus and had him flogged. And the soldiers wove a crown of thorns and put it on his head, and they dressed him in a purple robe. They kept coming up to him saying,
Soldier:	"Hail, King of the Jews!"
Narrator:	and striking him on the face. Pilate went out again and said to them,
Pilate:	"Look, I am bringing him out to you to let you know that I find no case against him."
Narrator:	So Jesus came out, wearing the crown of thorns and the purple robe. Pilate said to them,
Pilate:	"Here is the man!"
Narrator:	When the chief priests and the police saw him, they shouted,

Crowd **(choir):**	"Crucify him!" [*Repeat several times, with intensity*]
Narrator:	Pilate said to them,
Pilate:	"Take him yourselves and crucify him; I find no case against him."

(John 19:1-7)

Almost any passage of Scripture that includes dialogue lends itself to this kind of reading. When appropriate, print the reading in the bulletin and provide parts for the congregation.

9. *Use a reader's theater style of reading.* With this approach, the text is divided into several parts. For example, if reading the parable of the sower, consider having four different voices read the four different fates of the sower's seed. Most texts can be read in this fashion.

Voice 1:	The people that walked in darkness have seen a great light:
Voice 2:	They that dwell in the land of the shadow of death, upon them hath the light shined.
Voice 3:	For unto us a child is born,
Voice 4:	unto us a son is given:
Voice 3:	and the government shall be upon his shoulder:
Voice 4:	and his name shall be called
Voice 1:	Wonderful, Counsellor,
Voice 2:	The mighty God,
Voice 3:	The everlasting Father,
Voice 4:	The Prince of Peace.
Voice 1:	Of the increase of his government and peace
All:	there shall be no end. (Isa. 9:2, 6-7*a* KJV)

Although preparing reader's theater Scripture readings can be done quite easily, ready-made scripts are available. For example, Baker Book House publishes excellent resources, called *The Dramatized Old Testament* and *The Dramatized New Testament*, which arrange, in script format, passages from throughout the Bible.

10. *Read Scripture in conjunction with a song.* Scripture/music combinations can add great impact to the reading of

52

Holy Scripture. At times, they prove far more effective than a sermon. Consider this: At a Good Friday worship service, read selected passages from the passion narratives in Mark and Luke's Gospels. Between segments of the readings, a soloist might sing verses (a cappella) of "Were You There." The passages and hymn stanzas used could include

> ◇ Mark 14:22-24, 26-27, 29-37, 41-43, 45-46, 50
> [*Sing first stanza:* "*Were you there when they crucified my Lord?*"]
> ◇ Mark 14:53, 55, 60-65; 15:1, 12-20
> [*Sing second stanza:* "*Were you there when they nailed him to the tree?*"]
> ◇ Mark 15:25-32; Luke 23:34; Mark 15:33-34; Luke 23:46
> [*Sing third stanza:* "*Were you there when they laid him in the tomb?*"]

The above readings and solo should be preceded and/or followed by hymns or choruses focusing on the death of Christ. Traditional songs include "O Sacred Head, Now Wounded," "What Wondrous Love Is This," and "When I Survey the Wondrous Cross." A more contemporary example would be "Lamb of God."

11. *Occasionally let the Scripture readings serve as the sermon.* In some cases, the reading of extended passages of Scripture can take the place of a traditional sermon. The Good Friday service just mentioned is a good example. The same thing could be done at a Christmas Eve or Christmas Day worship service, using the following passages:

> ◇ the Annunciation to Mary (Luke 1:26-38)
> ◇ the Song of Elizabeth (Luke 1:39 45)
> ◇ the Magnificat of Mary (Luke 1:46-56)
> ◇ the Annunciation to Joseph (Matt. 1:18-25)
> ◇ the Birth of Jesus (Luke 2:1-7)
> ◇ the Praise of the Angels and Homage of the Shepherds (Luke 2:8-20)

For greater impact, intersperse appropriate music selections between the readings.

12. *Accompany a Scripture reading with liturgical movement.* Examples can be found in several resources (see appendix 2).

13. *Offer a dramatic monologue storytelling of the text.* Instead of reading a narrative text, occasionally tell the story from the perspective of one of the characters in the passage. For example, tell the story of Jesus healing the daughter of Jairus, but from the perspective of Jairus. Wearing a biblical costume adds to the storytelling.

14. *Present a slide presentation in conjunction with a Scripture reading.* Project nature slides while reading the Genesis story of creation. Another possibility is to purchase professional slides from the movie "Jesus of Nazareth" (see appendix 2 for more information). When reading texts from the life of Jesus, such as the Christmas story, the Lord's Supper, the Crucifixion, or the Resurrection, show the appropriate slides. They add to the reading of Scripture.

15. *Establish a lay readers team.* Every church has at least a few people who are effective readers. Pull together a group of these people and train them to implement some of the above suggestions.

Proclamation Through Drama

Drama can serve as a powerful means of proclamation during the service of the Word. Although an oversimplification, two major variations exist: drama presentations that *set up* the message, and drama presentations that *are* the message.

Drama Presentations That Set Up the Message

The most common use of drama in worship services is through brief sketches. Unlike a dramatic monologue or play, a drama sketch makes no attempt to adequately cover a subject. For the most part, drama sketches do not attempt to resolve a topic, they simply introduce a topic.

When preparing a worship service, I sometimes write a brief drama sketch to introduce the text and sermon. For example, while designing an eight-week worship series on the Lord's Prayer, my preparations included writing a brief drama sketch for each service. Some of the sketches were humorous, while others were serious. Here is the sketch for "thy kingdom come":

Read All About It

Three actors: one reader (male or female), and a couple.

Reader:	[*from pulpit*] "Our Father, who art in heaven, hallowed be thy name. Thy kingdom come . . . [*Pause*]
Wife:	What's in the news today, honey?
Husband:	[*holding paper*] Let's see, there is war in Bosnia, famine in North Korea, corruption in Washington. The national crime rate is up 15 percent. Drug use among junior high kids is increasing. Here's a story about police brutality, another story about a ten-car pileup on I-40 that killed eight people. Let's see what else there is . . .
Wife:	No, that's quite enough.
Reader:	Thy kingdom come . . . [*Pause*] Lord, will your kingdom ever come?

One Sunday while preaching a sermon on Christ's call to servanthood (Matt. 25:31-46), I used the following simple but effective drama sketch from *Drama for All Occasions* (pp. 43-45) based on this passage.

Being a Christian Servant

Seven characters. Note: Each interrupter stands where they are in the congregation to speak. When the leader continues, each interrupter may be seated. The element of surprise makes this most effective, especially with the first interrupter.

Leader: [*at the pulpit*] In the book of Matthew, we find a discussion about the final judgment and what being a Christian servant means. Listen reverently to these words from Matthew 25: "When the Son of Man comes as King and all the angels with him, he will sit on his royal throne, and the people of all the nations will be gathered before him. Then he will divide them into two groups, just as a shepherd separates the sheep from the goats. He will put the righteous people at his right and the others at his left. Then the King will say to the people on his right, "Come, you that are blessed by my Father! Come and possess the kingdom which has been prepared for you ever since the creation of the world. I was hungry and you fed me . . . I was . . ." (Matt. 25:31-35 TEV).

Interrupter 1: [*with intensity*] Wait just a minute, you didn't feed me. I was hungry and on the streets of _____. And I saw you drive right by me on your way to a fancy restaurant. You didn't even stop. No, you didn't feed me.

Leader: Excuse me, sir, but you are interrupting the reading of this Scripture. Please sit down and let me continue. "I was thirsty and you gave me a drink . . ." (Matt. 25:35*b* TEV).

Interrupter 2: Hey, you didn't give me a drink. In fact, you just ignored me on that hot day in June. My car had broken down on the interstate, and you just whizzed on by.

Leader: I'm sorry, but we don't have time for this. Verse 35, "I was a stranger and you received me in your homes . . ."

Interrupter 3: Boy, that's a joke. I came to visit your church and you were too busy visiting with your own little group. You didn't even take the time to say hello much less invite me to your home.

Leader: Don't you have any reverence for the Word of God? Please allow me to continue, "I was naked and you clothed me . . ." (Matt. 25:36 TEV).

Interrupter 4: I wish you could know how embarrassing it is to wear the same clothes day after day after day. After a while, it begins to wear down your

	dignity. I just wish you could know what it feels like.
Leader:	I'm sorry, but these people don't want to hear about your problems. They've got problems of their own. Besides, they came to listen to this Scripture. Verse 36 says, "I was sick and you took care of me . . ."
Interrupter 5:	I'm afraid you didn't take care of me. I was put in a nursing home, and the only times you came to visit me were on Christmas and Easter. Where were you the rest of the year?
Leader:	I'm afraid these interruptions are taking away from the Scriptures. Please listen. "I was in prison and you visited me . . ." (Matt. 25:36 TEV).
Interrupter 6:	Prison is a lonely place. I ought to know, I was there for a year and felt like a number. I don't think anybody cared about what happened to me in there.
Leader:	"The righteous will then answer him, 'When, Lord, did we ever see you hungry and feed you, or thirsty and give you a drink? When did we ever see you a stranger and welcome you in our homes, or naked and clothe you? When did we ever see you sick or in prison, and visit you?' The King will reply, 'I tell you, whenever you did this for one of the least important of these brothers of mine, you did it for me!' Then he will say to those on his left, 'God's curse! Away to the eternal fire which has been prepared for the Devil and his angels! I was hungry but you would not feed me . . .' "
	(Matt. 25:37-42*a* TEV).
Interrupter 1:	Yeah, that's right. I just needed a good hot meal. [*Stands and remains standing until the end*]
Leader:	" 'Thirsty but you would not give me a drink . . .' "
	(Matt. 25:42*b* TEV).
Interrupter 2:	All I needed was a helping hand and a cool drink of water. [*Stands and remains standing*]
Leader:	" 'I was a stranger but you would not welcome me in your homes . . .' " (Matt. 25:43*a* TEV).

Interrupter 3:	Just a simple hello would have been a start. [*Stands*]
Leader:	" 'Naked but you would not clothe me . . .' " (Matt. 25:43*b* TEV).
Interrupter 4:	All I needed was a clean dress and a little respect. [*Stands*]
Leader:	" 'I was sick . . .' "
Interrupter 5:	I just needed someone to be there. [*Stands*]
Leader:	" 'And in prison but you would not take care of me . . .' " (Matt. 25:43*c* TEV).
Interrupter 6:	I just wanted a friend to help fill the loneliness. [*Stands*]
Leader:	"Then they will answer him, 'When, Lord, did we ever see you hungry or thirsty or a stranger or naked or sick or in prison, and we would not help you?' The King will reply, 'I tell you, whenever you refused to help one of these least important ones, you refused to help me.' These, then, will be sent off to eternal punishment, but the righteous will go to eternal life" (Matt. 25:44-46 TEV). [*Pause; realization*] Oh my goodness, I think I understand now. [*Pause*] Forgive me, Lord. [*Bows head; freeze*]

Several years ago, on All Saints Day, I preached a sermon on the hope of eternal life. To set up the theme for the congregation, the following simple drama sketch was presented.

Reader:	[*from pulpit*] Around 1800, a child named John Todd was born in Vermont. When John was six, both his mother and father died, and his brothers and sisters had to be divided up among various relatives. John was sent to live with his aunt, whom he had never met. She loved and nurtured him, and then sent him to college. When John was a grown man, he received word that his aunt was terrified at the thought of her impending death. Although John wanted to go to her, it was impossible at the time. Instead, he wrote her a letter.

A man enters from the side and takes a seat at a table. Lights dim, and a spotlight focuses on him. He takes out a pen and paper and begins to write a letter. As he writes, a voice (offstage) reads:

Reader 2:   [*offstage*] My dearest aunt Evelyn: Thirty-five years ago, when my parents died, I was left all alone in the world. I have never forgotten the day that I made the long journey to your house in North Killingsworth. I remember feeling disappointed that instead of coming for me yourself, you sent your servant, Caesar, to pick me up. Caesar placed me on the back of his horse, and I held his waist tightly, full of fear and fighting back tears. As we headed for my new home, I became more and more frightened. I finally asked Caesar, "Do you think she will be asleep when we arrive? "Don't worry," said Caesar reassuringly, "she will stay awake for you. When we pass this part of the woods, you will be able to see her candle in the window." A few minutes later we rode into a clearing; sure enough, your candle was burning in the window. I'll never forget that moment. You were waiting at the door for me. You smiled at me, put your arms around me, and lifted me down from the horse. Inside a fire was roaring in the fireplace, and a warm dinner was waiting for me on the stove. After dinner, you took me to bed, heard my prayers, and held my hand until I fell asleep. Surely you know why I am telling you this story. Someday soon God may send for you, to take you to a new home. Don't fear the strange journey toward death, for at the end of the road you will find love and welcome. You will be safe in death, just as you have been in life; you will be in God's love and care. Surely God will be as loving and kind to you as you were to me those many years ago. With love and affection, John.

After a moment of silence, the man leaves the table, and a soloist begins to sing a cappella the old hymn "Shall We Gather at the River."

The sermon followed.

Drama Presentations That Are the Message

Drama can occasionally serve *as* the message rather than a tool that sets up the message. Examples include one-act plays, Christmas or Easter dramas, dramatic monologues, or extended stories. Two examples follow: a story sermon and a dramatic monologue.

1. *A story sermon.* An extended story can sometimes serve as the sermon. Biblical precedence for this approach abounds. For example, when Jesus wanted to communicate the love and grace of God, he did not say, "Let me share three principles about God's love." Instead, our Lord said, "There once was a man who had two sons. . . ."

Recently, I prepared a service of the Word based—once again—on Matthew 25:31-46. Lay readers read the text in a reader's theater style, using the script provided in the *Dramatized New Testament* (see appendix 2). After another Scripture reading, a choral anthem, and a congregational chorus called "Make Me a Servant," I told the following story. The story did not support, illustrate, or set up the sermon; the story *was* the sermon.

At the beginning of the sixteenth century, when the Jews were expelled from Spain, they went all over: France, Germany, Greece, and some went to the Holy Land. Among them was Jacoby. He was a shoemaker by trade. Jacoby was a kind man, but the thing that everybody noticed about him was that he was so devout. He would go to the synagogue every Sabbath and listen to what the rabbi was saying, and that was odd because Jacoby spoke Spanish and the rabbi spoke Hebrew. But Jacoby would screw up his face and listen and listen, trying to catch every word.

One Sabbath, the rabbi gave a sermon and mentioned how loaves of bread were offered to God when the holy temple was still there. Jacoby heard "bread" and he heard "God" and he got so excited. He ran home and said to his wife, "Esperanza! Guess what! God eats bread! And you are the best baker in the whole country! This week make your best bread, and I will take it to God."

That week Esperanza kneaded in the best ingredients, and with her best intentions she braided the bread with such love. The next week Jacoby took seven loaves of bread to the synagogue.

"Señor Dios. I've got your bread. You'll see, you'll love it. My wife, Esperanza—she's a wonderful baker! You'll eat every crumb!" And with that he took the bread and put it into the holy ark.

No sooner did he leave than in came the shammes, the man who cleans up the synagogue. "Lord, you know I want to be here in this holy place; that's all I want to do. But for seven weeks now I haven't been paid. Lord, I need for you to make me a miracle. I believe you're going to; maybe you have done it already. Maybe I'll open the holy ark and there will be my miracle." And he walked to the ark and opened it up, and there was his miracle. Seven loaves of bread! Enough for the whole week.

The next day when the rabbi opened up the ark, and Jacoby and Esperanza saw that the bread was gone, you should have seen the look of love that passed between them.

The next week it was the same. And the week after, it was the same. This went on for months and months. The shammes learned to have faith in God. But if he hung around the synagogue or came too early, no miracle.

And so, thirty years went by. Thirty years later, Jacoby came to the synagogue with his loaves of bread. "Señor Dios, I know your bread's been lumpy lately. Esperanza's arthritis . . . maybe you could do something? You'll eat better!" He put the bread in the ark and started to leave when suddenly the rabbi grabbed him.

"What are you doing?" the rabbi asked. Jacoby said, "I'm bringing God his bread." The rabbi said, "God doesn't eat bread!" Jacoby said, "He's been eating Esperanza's bread for thirty years." The two men heard a noise, and they hid.

No sooner did they hide than in came the shammes. "I hate to bring it up, Lord, but you know, your bread's been lumpy lately. Maybe you could talk to an angel." Then the shammes reached in the ark to get the bread, and suddenly the rabbi jumped out and grabbed him.

The rabbi began to yell at the two men, telling them how sinful it was that they were doing this, and going on and on. All three men began to cry. Jacoby began to cry because he only wanted to do good. The rabbi began to cry because all of this happened because of a sermon. And the shammes began to cry because suddenly he knew there was going to be no more bread.

Suddenly they heard laughter in the corner. They turned, and it was the great mystic, Rabbi Isaac. He was shaking his head and laughing and said, "No, rabbi, these men—they are not sinful. These men are devout! You should know that God has never had more pleasure, or more fun, than watching what goes on in your synagogue. On the Sabbath, he sits with his angels and they laugh, watching this man bring the bread and the other man take the bread, and God gets all the credit! You must beg forgiveness of these men, rabbi."

And then he looked at Jacoby and said, "Jacoby, you must do something even more difficult. You must now bring your bread directly to the shammes; and when you do, you must believe with perfect faith that it is the same as giving it to God."

Sounds a lot like another rabbi named Jesus, who said, "to the extent that you did it unto the least of these, you did it unto me" (Matt. 25:40 paraphrased).

2. *A dramatic monologue.* Once or twice a year a dramatic monologue can be presented in place of a traditional sermon. Although the following monologue was written for Holy Week, it can be used at any time during the year. The monologue is based on John 13:1-15.

He Took a Towel

Note: Walk in from the back of the sanctuary. Carry a towel and a wash basin. A costume, such as a white alb with no stole, makes the sermon more effective.

Good morning. My name is John. I was one of Jesus' disciples. I would like to tell you about some of my experiences with Jesus. You are probably wondering why I brought a towel and wash basin. Let me explain.

I remember one night in particular, many years ago. It was the time of Passover, and Jesus wanted his disciples to celebrate it together. We met in an upper room in Jerusalem. During the meal, Jesus rose from the table, gathered a wash basin like this one, poured out some water, and began to wash our feet. We could hardly believe it. Here was our Master, our Lord, and he was acting like a common servant. It was extremely awkward. Jesus came to Peter. Peter said what we were all thinking. He said, "No Lord, you should not wash my feet!" It seemed so out of place, so wrong. But Jesus insisted that he do so. As we sat in silence while Jesus washed our feet, I began to think about what was happening. Here was our Lord, the Christ, the Son of God, acting like a common slave and washing our feet. And yet, as I thought about it, it was not so strange after all. In a sense, he was always washing the feet of others. He was always a servant, always meeting the needs of people.

The thing that most impressed me about Jesus was his deep compassion and love for people. He cared about people and ministered to their needs.

Jesus cared about people's physical needs. One day we were passing through Jericho. A blind man named Bartimaeus cried out for help. At first I paid him no mind; he was just another blind beggar. But he kept on shouting, "Son of David, have mercy on me!" Jesus heard him shouting. He stopped and walked over to him. Jesus touched his eyes and healed him.

Jesus often helped people who were sick. He healed the blind, the lame, and the mentally ill. I remember when a man with leprosy came to Jesus for help. All the disciples were upset. Nobody wanted to get close to a leper. As we watched, Jesus actually touched this man. We could hardly believe our eyes. Jesus loved him and cared about his suffering. When Jesus touched him, his leprosy went away.

There was a time when five thousand people gathered to hear Jesus teach. The day had come to an end, and everyone was hungry. We advised Jesus to send them away. But he said, "Give them something to eat." And with two fish and five loaves of bread, he fed the whole crowd. He often met the physical needs of people.

Jesus also cared about people's emotional needs. He had compassion for those who grieved and for those who were depressed, discouraged, or confused. Many times Jesus helped his own disciples when we were emotionally upset. I remember one time in particular. It was after Jesus had been killed and resurrected. He was talking to Peter. Peter felt badly about having denied Jesus three times. Jesus said to Peter, "Do you love me?" It hurt Peter because he had failed him. But Peter did love Jesus and said, "Yes, Lord, I love you." Then Jesus asked him a second time, and then a third. Peter was grieved but said for the third time, "Yes, Lord, I love you." After this was over we all realized what Jesus had done. Peter had denied Jesus three times. And now Jesus had given him the opportunity to reaffirm his love three times. Afterwards, Peter and Jesus embraced. I heard Jesus say to Peter, "Peter, I love you, and I forgive you." It was a healing event for Peter. He gained much strength from it. Jesus often met the emotional needs of people.

Jesus also cared about people's spiritual needs. More than anything else, Jesus wanted people to know God. I remember the night Nicodemus came to see Jesus. Jesus told him that he needed to be born again. Jesus was teaching him that people need spiritual life and renewal that only God could provide.

For three years I followed Jesus. I saw him care about people again and again. He ministered to their needs, whether they were physical, emotional, or spiritual in nature. And he constantly taught us to do the same. He told us that if we wanted to be great we must be servants. He told us over and over, "Care about people; minister to their needs."

I thought of these things that night as Jesus washed our feet. It was a strange night, a scary night. Jesus took bread and wine and said they represented his body and blood, which would be broken and shed for us. He spoke of dying. We did not understand. After supper we went up on the mountain. Jesus was deeply distressed. He asked Peter, James, and me to pray with him. He was in great agony. We were so tired, however, that we fell asleep. We woke to the sound of Roman soldiers. It was a nightmare. Jesus was arrested, and we all ran like scared animals.

We kept up with the situation the best we could. We learned that Jesus was being seen by various officials and he was on trial. Then the word came: Jesus was to be crucified. We could not believe it. Why? Because he loved? I felt that my life was caving in all around me. All my hopes and dreams were invested in Jesus, and now they were going to kill him. He was mocked and beaten and finally led to Golgotha. We were hiding, afraid that we might be next.

Mary, the mother of Jesus, came to me and asked if I would take her to Jesus. I said no at first. I tried to explain that it was a horrible sight to see a man crucified. I was also worried that the officials might recognize us. But Mary persisted, and I finally gave in. As we arrived at the execution site, I felt sick to my stomach. It was a gruesome and horrible scene. Death was everywhere. The people were mocking Jesus, and the Roman soldiers were laughing and having a great time. I was filled with hatred and anger. I was also angry at myself for having failed my Lord. I wanted Jesus to kill them all—the entire, hate-filled crowd. And I knew he had the power to do it but that he would not.

We moved a little closer to the cross where Jesus hung. He was talking. I could barely make out what he said. It was hard to believe what Jesus was saying. He said, "Father, forgive them." Those animals were killing Jesus, and he was asking God to forgive them!

In spite of his pain and agony, Jesus took time to speak to the man on the cross next to him. He assured the man that he could be forgiven and would be with God in paradise that very day. Jesus was still meeting the needs of people, all the way to the end. Then Jesus looked directly at me. I felt ashamed. I had run away and deserted him when the soldiers came. And yet his eyes were filled with love. He also looked at his mother, Mary, who was weeping. Then he said to me, "Behold your mother!" He then looked at Mary and said, "Behold your son!" We knew exactly what he was doing. He was making provisions for his mother. He was caring for her needs even as he was dying.

In those last moments all Jesus thought about was others. He was concerned about the people who were killing him, about the thief next to him, and about his mother. He was a servant to the end, caring for people and meeting their needs in his death, even as he did in life. He was the man for others, the servant of all. Once again he had a towel in his hands, and he was washing the feet of others.

Of course you know the story. After the darkness of the cross, God raised Jesus from the dead. And then Jesus established his church to continue his ministry through the ages. Yet I will never forget that night in the upper room when Jesus, the Christ, the Son of God, got down on his hands and knees and washed our feet. And as he did he taught us a great lesson. "As I have done to you," he said, "so you should do to others." Although he was the Christ, he carried a towel in his hands and washed the feet of others. When I think of that night, I recall the words he often said, "Go and do likewise."

(Martin Thielen)

A large and growing number of worship drama resources are readily available from a variety of sources, including most denominational publishing houses and Christian bookstores. See appendix 2 for a list of sources.

Media Presentations

We live in an increasingly visually oriented, "postliterate" age. Young people do not listen to music anymore, they watch it. A growing number of churches now use media presentations in their worship services. Many pastors use short movie clips to introduce or illustrate their sermons. For example, a pastor preaching a sermon on what it means to be successful might consider using a video clip from the movie *Eight Seconds*. The film tells the story of a young, rising rodeo star. In one scene, his mother points to all his father's rodeo trophies and asks, "What do you see when you look at all those trophies?" The young man, who is becoming consumed with success at the expense of his marriage, does not answer. His mother says, "I see dust."

One pastor took his camcorder to the local mall and asked

people to look into the camera and answer the question, "Who is Jesus Christ to you?" As you might expect, he received an interesting variety of responses. He edited the tape and used it as the introduction to his sermon the following Sunday. Of course, if a church wants to use video in its service, the church will need to invest in a video projection machine, or, if the sanctuary is small, a large-screen television.

Another medium is the use of slides. As already mentioned, slides can be used in the gathering and during the reading of Scripture. However, they can also be used to enhance the sermon. For example, I once used a slide presentation to conclude a sermon on evangelism. Several weeks before the sermon, I asked a college student in my congregation to wander around the city and take slides of different kinds of people. At the end of my sermon, the slides were projected onto a large screen while a soloist sang "People Need the Lord." It proved to be a powerful conclusion to the sermon.

In his provocative book *Out on the Edge: A Wake-up Call for Church Leaders on the Edge of the Media Reformation* (Nashville: Abingdon Press, 1998), Michael Slaughter writes that "the Media Reformation is a life or death issue for the church" (p. 25). He argues that "we can no longer afford to pursue our ministry in the old, tired, linear, literate way. The sight-and-sound generation calls for a multisensory experience" (p. 36). Throughout the book, he offers specific examples of using media in worship and includes a CD-ROM on multisensory worship.

The Sermon

Most of my sermons are narrative, "storytelling" sermons. Simply put, story preaching is fundamentally storytelling in its methodology. A story sermon may take the form of an extended biblical story, which moves the listener from "once upon a time" to "happily ever after." However, story sermons are often a combination of several stories, both biblical and nonbiblical. An example of the multistory method is found in Luke 15, where Jesus told stories about a lost sheep, a lost coin, and a lost son. Although the heart of a story sermon is a biblical narrative, story preaching also uses stories from history, literature, theater, motion pictures, current events, and personal experiences. This is my primary mode of preaching, because story preaching

- ◇ is congruent with the biblical record.
- ◇ follows the example of Jesus.
- ◇ touches the heart.
- ◇ is effective in a visual age.
- ◇ captures and holds the congregation's attention.
- ◇ makes the sermon memorable.
- ◇ gives movement to the sermon.
- ◇ takes seriously right brain/left brain research.
- ◇ eliminates the need for a manuscript and reduces the need for notes.
- ◇ makes an impact.

An example of an *extended-story sermon* can be found in chapter 7. This story sermon about Pastor Stephens was originally written for the opening worship service of a preaching and worship conference. Later, the sermon was used as part of a series of sermons on the five primary tasks of the church: worship, evangelism, discipleship, ministry, and fellowship.

An example of a *multistory sermon* follows. The original idea and much of the content comes from a sermon Fred Craddock preached several years ago called, "When the Roll Is Called Down Here." The sermon, which is basically a string of stories, is based on Romans 16:1-16, which was read immediately before the sermon.

More Than a List

Aren't you glad you didn't have to read today's text? This passage of Scripture is nothing more than a list of names—hard-to-pronounce names at that. Names of people who belonged to the church in Rome during Paul's day. And reading a list of names is not very exciting. So don't feel guilty if your heart was not strangely warmed during the reading of this text. Yet, right here in Holy Scripture, the apostle Paul writes out a list of names. Just one name after another after another. Pretty boring passage. It's just a list.

But Paul would be offended if you referred to it as a mere list. You see, it was far more than a list to him. Perhaps we could better understand if we could go to Washington, D.C., and see the Vietnam Memorial. It's just a list of names. Block after block of names, Vietnam names. Some people go to the memorial and see a list of names, nothing more. But for others it's much more than a list. If you went there, you might see a woman put her finger on a name, and then hold up a child and put the child's hand on the name. You might see another woman kiss one of the names on the wall. You might see a man wearing a military jacket find the name of an old friend and touch it and weep. You would see many flowers on the ground. Now I ask you, is the Vietnam Memorial a list of names? Yes, it is, but it's much more than a list.

Romans 16 is Paul's list. These were people who helped Paul through some hard times in his life. Look at this list again. In verse 3 we read about Aquila and Priscilla. They risked their necks for Paul. In verse 5, Paul speaks of his dear friend Epaenetus, his first convert in Asia. In verse 6 he tells about Mary, who works hard for the Lord. In verse 7, he lists Andronicus and Junia, who spent time in prison with Paul. In verse 9, Paul speaks of his dear friend Stachys. In verse 12 he lists Tryphaena and Tryphosa, twins, women who work hard in the church. He also mentions his dear friend Persis. Look at verse 13. He lists Rufus and Rufus's mother, who was like a mother to Paul. (Can you imagine a woman being a mother to the apostle Paul? Can't you just hear her say, "Now Paul, I don't care if you are an apostle, you have to eat your breakfast"?)

So many names on the list. But don't you see, this is more than a list to Paul. These people meant the world to him. And I think I understand something about Paul's list. You see, I have a list of my own. Years ago, when I was leaving a church, the congregation threw us a good-bye reception. All those who came signed a guest book. I got it out and looked at it not long ago. It's just a list of people's names.

People like Mable, the church secretary. Mable has been secretary of that church since creation. When I first came to the church, Mable asked me, "Brother Martin, how old are you?" "Twenty-five," I replied. I knew better than to ask how old she was, so I asked her, "How long have you been secretary here?" "Twenty-*six* years," she said. Mable, my grandmother in the faith!

Randall's name was also on the list. Randall, our one-armed music minister. I must admit, I was reluctant to go to a church where the music minister only had one arm. But after a while you never noticed. Randall could even tie a necktie with one hand.

There were other names. Like Steve, a dentist and perhaps the best church friend I've ever had. Or Jim, who voted against every salary increase I ever received. Or Ralph, the plumber. The first week I was at the church we had a plumbing problem. I asked somebody whom to call. "Ralph," they said. "What's his number?" "He doesn't have a phone." "Where is his office?" "He doesn't have an office." "How do you find him?" "You drive around town and look for his little blue pickup truck and ask him to come over."

Or Larry the lawyer. He always called me "preacher" so I started calling him "lawyer." Larry always said, "Preacher, feel free to let your hair down around me." Of course, I had a lot more of it to let down back then. Or Lynda, only forty-two but already a widow. I buried her husband a few months before I left the church. He died of a rare heart disorder. Lots of names on this list, but it's so much more than a list to me.

Who is on your list? Who knows you and all of your faults but loves you anyway? Or who has helped you through a hard time? A divorce, or a death, or a medical problem, or a broken dream, or a personal failure? Do you have a list of people who are important to you. I hope so.

Tell you what—let's do something different here. Get out a piece of paper; use your worship bulletin, if you want. I want you to write a list of your own, your own Romans 16. You certainly don't have to. Nobody will know if you do or don't and nobody but you will see it. But if you are willing, write down the names of the really important people in your life. Take a minute and write a name or two, or three, or five.

While you are writing, let me tell you about Carol's list. Carol was a member of a church I used to serve. Carol is a wonderful woman, full of life and joy. But Carol's eighteen-year-old son was killed in a car wreck a few years ago. It's a long sad story that I don't need to tell today, but about six or eight weeks after his death, Carol brought me an article for the church newsletter. It was basically a list. She wanted to thank some people in the church for their support during that horrible time. People like Susan, who came right over and answered the phone and called all the relatives with the bad news. And Judy, who stayed at Carol's house for almost a week cleaning house and cooking and keeping things going. And Charles, who came over and mowed the lawn for several months after the death. And Jo, who also lost a son a few years earlier. Jo just came and sat and cried with Carol. She understood. "Thank you," said Carol to these people and several others. Just a list of names. Not very interesting if you were reading the church newsletter and didn't know who these people were or what they did. But to Carol, it was far more than a list. It was the names of the people who helped her survive the worst nightmare of her life.

They have a name for that sort of thing back where I come from in Arkansas. They call it church family. Indeed, Carol began her list by saying, "Dear church family."

So, have you finished your list yet? Do you have a name or two or three or five? I hope so. If not on paper then in your heart. And if you do have a list, you had better hang on to it. Don't lose it. You may lose your money or your health or your career or your dreams, but don't lose your list. Never. Keep it forever. If you move, keep it. No matter what happens, keep the list and keep adding names to it. In fact, when your life is over and you leave this earth, take the list with you.

I know, I know, when you get to the gate, St. Peter's going to say, "Now look, you have to understand the rules up here. You went into the world with nothing and you have to come out of it with nothing. What do you have in your hand?"

And you will say, "Well, it's just a list of names." And Peter will say, "Let me see it."

"Well, this is just some names of folks who have helped me."

"Let me see it."

"Well, this is just a group of people that if it weren't for them, I'd have never made it."

Peter will say, "I want to see it."

So you give it to him. He smiles and says, "I know all of these people. In fact, on my way here to meet you at the gate, I passed a whole group of them. They were painting a big red sign to hang over the street. It said, 'Welcome home.' "

(Martin Thielen)

Although I am an advocate of story preaching, not every sermon needs to be a storytelling sermon. Even an effective method, if used all the time, grows old. The Bible, which is mostly narrative, is not all narrative. Therefore occasionally I preach traditional, "point" sermons. When I do, I prepare a listening guide for the congregation that helps people stay more focused and attentive to the sermon. The guide is either printed in the bulletin or is included as an insert.

An example of a listening guide appears below. The blanks in the guide are for the congregation to fill in as the sermon unfolds. The congregation is invited to read the printed Scripture references along with the preacher. This particular sermon was the first in a series of sermons on the book of Ecclesiastes called "Secrets of Life." In this opening sermon, four diversionary paths that Ecclesiastes traveled in his quest for the good life are pointed out. These paths were not wrong or unimportant, they were simply inadequate. The four paths are not the secrets of life and are not worthy of our ultimate concern.

1. The path of _____.
"I said to myself, 'I have acquired great wisdom, sur-passing all who were over Jerusalem before me; and my mind has had great experience of wisdom and knowl-edge.' " (1:16)

2. The path of _____.
"I said to myself, 'Come now, I will make a test of pleasure; enjoy yourself.' " (2:1)

3. The path of _____.
"I bought male and female slaves, and had slaves who were born in my house; I also had great posses-sions of herds and flocks, more than any who had been before me in Jerusalem. I also gathered for myself silver and gold and the treasure of kings and of the provinces." (2:7-8)

4. The path of _____.
"I made great works; I built houses and planted vine-yards for myself; I made myself gardens and parks, and planted in them all kinds of fruit trees." (2:4-5)

The four paths were (1) philosophy, (2) pleasure, (3) pos-sessions, and (4) production (career advancement, success, and personal accomplishments). Other sermons in the series pointed out that a quality life was balanced (Eccl. 3:1-8), focused on the present moment (Eccl. 9:3-10), centered on relationships (Eccl. 4:7-12), and grounded in faith (Eccl. 12:1-7, 13).

Telling stories and using listening guides are a way to help make sermons more interactive for listeners. Another way to engage the congregation is to occasionally ask them questions during the sermon. During a sermon on the kingdom of God that used a section of the Lord's Prayer— "your kingdom come . . . on earth as it is in heaven"—I asked the congregation, "If the kingdom of God were to come on earth, what would it look like?" People responded: "There would be no more war." "Cancer would be cured." "All homeless people would have a place to live." "Crime would end." "Pollution would be nonexistent." This time of interaction only took a few moments, but it added greatly to the sermon.

Although I enjoy preaching and believe in its importance, the sermon is only one part of the entire worship event. Therefore, when preparing for Sunday, I prepare for the whole service and not just the sermon. As a result, my sermons are typically brief, and last about twelve to seventeen minutes. The benefits of shorter sermons are significant.

- ◇ The congregation's attention is better retained.
- ◇ The sermons are more focused.
- ◇ Only the best materials on that particular topic are used.
- ◇ Plenty of time is left for other, equally important aspects of the worship service.

There is a growing uneasiness among some pastors about the current homiletic trend, especially in contemporary churches, toward need-based, practical advice-giving, therapeutic preaching. Although forgetting human needs in preaching is not advisable, many churches have gone overboard. A review of recent sermons at several high-profile contemporary churches illustrated the large number of sermons that constantly focus on topics such as marriage, parenting, building better relationships, managing stress, financial management, overcoming anxiety, and being successful in the marketplace. This type of preaching may have the tendency to produce a self-centered, narcissistic generation of believers, and promotes a human-centered rather than God-centered experience of worship. Ultimately, people come to church to encounter the living Lord, not helpful hints for being successful, or personal therapy advice. Success suggestions and therapy are available elsewhere; however, worship is not. Therefore, more sermons on the transcendence of God; the life, death, and resurrection of Christ; the work of the Spirit; the life of prayer; the historic doctrines of the church; and Christ's summons to service and discipleship are needed. In short, we need sermons and worship services that are focused more on God and less on ourselves.

Other Acts of Proclamation

Scripture readings, drama, media presentations, and sermons do not exhaust the possibilities for proclamation in worship; consider also the following.

1. *Liturgical movement.* As I mentioned in chapter 2, a growing number of churches are using liturgical movement in their worship services. In many instances, liturgical movement can be an appropriate and deeply moving addition to the service of the Word. Consider the following example, based on Psalm 36:

[*To be done in pairs (or one pair) by an even number of persons*]

How precious is thy steadfast love, O God!
[*Take partners and spread out. One member of each pair begins by kneeling, or sitting back on his or her heels, body bent over; the other begins by standing, facing the partner. Hold this position while the first line is slowly read. Then in response the person kneeling raises his or her back and lifts up his or her hands, palms upward, as the standing person (a "God figure" of love) bends forward and lowers the hands, palms downward, till*]

73

they meet the upraised hands of the partner. This is done very slowly, so that the meeting of the hands becomes a meaningful moment.]

The children of men and women take refuge in the shadow of thy wings.
[*While the line is read, the lower person in each set rises to his or her knees and each couple then slowly embraces, folding arms around one another.*]

They feast on the abundance of thy house.
[*The "God figure" helps the kneeling person to rise, then grasps with the right hand the partner's left hand and steps backward in a small circle as the partner walks forward. The "God figure" leads the other gently around, gestures with the free hand as if showing the "house"—the river of delights. Think of it as a thanksgiving in movement for God's bounty.*]

And thou givest them drink from the river of thy delights.
[*The "God figure" bends down as if scooping imaginary water and rising, passes it to the partner who with cupped hands and swaying body accepts it in a variety of ways (such as drinking deeply, bathing in a fountain, and so on). This passing and receiving can be done a number of times.*]

For with thee is the fountain of delight.
[*Both persons gradually stop the gesture and come to a standing position facing each other, a few feet apart. Both persons place their hands with palms facing inward, a few inches in front of their own face.*]

In thy light do we see light.
[*All slowly separate their hands as if parting a curtain, and look at their partner face-to-face, receiving "light" from one another. This position is held for a few seconds.*]

(*The Complete Library of Christian Worship*, vol. 4, p. 761)

2. *Poetry and other readings.* During a stewardship Sunday, I once used a Michel Quoist reading, "Prayer Before a Twenty-Dollar Bill," as the introduction to our service of the Word.

Lord, see this bill! It frightens me.
You know its secrets, you know its history.
How heavy it is!

It scares me, for it cannot speak.
It will never tell all it hides in its creases.
It will never reveal all the struggles and efforts it represents, all
the disillusionment and slighted dignity.
It is stained with sweat and blood,
It is laden with all the weight of the human toil which makes its
worth.
It is heavy, heavy, Lord.
It fills me with awe, it frightens me.
For it has death on its conscience . . .
All the poor fellows who killed themselves for it,
To possess it for a few hours,
To have through it a little pleasure, a little joy, a little life.
Through how many hands has it passed, Lord?
And what has it done in the course of its long, silent journeys?
It has offered white roses to the radiant fiancée.
It has paid for the baptismal party, and fed the rosy-cheeked
baby.
It has provided bread for the family table.
Because of it there was laughing among the young and joy
among the elders.
It has paid for the saving visit of the doctor,
It has bought the book that taught the youngster,
It has clothed the young girl.
But it has sent the letter breaking the engagement,
It has paid for the death of the baby in its mother's womb,
It has bought the liquor that made the drunkard,
It has produced the movie unfit for children,
And has recorded the indecent song.
It has broken the morals of the adolescent and made of the adult a
thief.
It has bought for a few hours the body of a woman.
It has paid for the weapons of the crime and for the wood of the
coffin.
O Lord, I offer you this bill with its joyous mysteries, its sor-
rowful mysteries.
I thank you for all the life and joy it has given.
I ask your forgiveness for the harm it has done.
But above all, Lord, I offer it to you as a symbol of all the labors
of men, indestructible money, which tomorrow will be
changed into your eternal life.

3. *Visual arts.* The visual arts, which include stained-
glass windows, wood and stone carvings, tapestries, paint-
ings and vestments, have been used in Christian worship for

centuries. In recent years, a growing number of churches have begun using banners as a means of proclamation. Solicit a group of retirees who like to sew, and ask them to make beautiful banners that will enhance the worship service. Enlist their help in creating banners for Communion, Thanksgiving, Advent and Christmas, or other special days in the life of the church. A good resource for a beginning banner ministry is *Banners for Worship* (see appendix 2).

Of course, visual arts include far more than banners. Consider also the use of vestments, candles, flowers, stained glass, sculpture, and other expressions of visual art.

4. *Testimonies.* Occasionally ask people in the congregation to share some aspect of their faith experience during the service of the Word. They could share how they came to Christ, or how they came to the church, or how God sustained them through a difficult time, or their experience in one of the various ministries of the church.

5. *Music.* Music can be effectively interspersed throughout the service of the Word. For example, musical selections (anthems, ensembles, solos, hymns, choruses, or instrumental music) can be used

- ◇ before the Scripture readings.
- ◇ between Scripture readings.
- ◇ as a Scripture reading (if the text is set to music).
- ◇ before, during, or after a drama sketch.
- ◇ before, during, or after a sermon (An anthem, solo, chorus or hymn can be used to conclude a sermon).
- ◇ in conjunction with a liturgical dance.
- ◇ in conjunction with a media presentation.

Chapter 4

We Respond to the Call of God

After gathering to worship God and listening to the Word of God, worshipers are prepared to respond to the call of God. This time of response has been a vital part of worship since biblical times. Take Isaiah, for example. After affirming the glory of God and after hearing the Word of God, Isaiah responded to the call of God by saying, "Here am I; scnd me" (Isa. 6:8*b*).

It is important to remember that worship is not a spectator event. Indeed, the congregation should be the primary participants in the act of worship. Unfortunately, some contemporary churches utilize a nonparticipatory style of worship. These worship services, sometimes called "seeker services," focus more on a performance rather than a participatory model of worship.

Blended worship stands in stark contrast to nonparticipatory worship services. Although blended worship makes use of some seeker-service methodologies, the third movement of worship, "We Respond to the Call of God," is a central component of a blended service. Many different responses to God's call upon our life can be made during this third portion of the worship service. Consider these possibilities:

- ◇ an initial commitment to Christ
- ◇ baptism
- ◇ reaffirmation of baptism vows

◇ confirmation
◇ moving of church membership
◇ anointing with oil for healing and wholeness
◇ passing of the peace
◇ giving of an offering
◇ reciting the Nicene or Apostles' Creed, or some other affirmation of faith
◇ songs of dedication and faith
◇ prayers of various kinds
◇ commissioning of lay leaders for various acts of service

Many congregations observe the following responses to God's call on a weekly basis:

1. God's call to faith
2. God's call to prayer
3. God's call to stewardship
4. God's call to community

Suggestions for planning these responses are detailed below.

God's Call to Faith

The first congregational response after the service of the Word can be called "God's call to faith." At least five responses can be made during this movement of worship.

◇ invitation to discipleship
◇ song of response
◇ affirmation of faith
◇ baptism
◇ renewal of baptism vows

1. *Invitation to discipleship.* Following the service of the Word, the congregation can be invited to Christian discipleship. This invitation can take numerous forms. Many congregations extend a public invitation after the sermon, inviting people to affirm faith in Christ or to become a member of the church, and it is usually accompanied by a song of invitation. Traditional invitation songs include "Just As I Am" and "Softly and Tenderly Jesus Is Calling," while "Change My Heart, O God" and "O Lord, Your Tenderness" are examples of contemporary invitation songs. Although a valid method of responding to God's call, public invitations were not a part of Christian worship until the frontier camp meetings of the early 1800s, and are not necessary for authentic worship to occur. Instead of a public invitation to "walk the aisle," a growing number of contemporary churches ask people to make commitments through the use of decision cards. Persons mark the cards indicating that they want more information on becoming a Christian or a church member, place the card in the offering plate, and a pastor or lay minister calls or visits during the following week. Still other churches provide counseling centers where people can go after the worship service to discuss spiritual issues. Of course, many churches do none of the above. Persons in these congregations simply share their spiritual decisions with their minister, who later presents them for baptism or church membership.

2. *Song of response.* Many, if not most, churches sing a song of response immediately following the sermon. This can be an invitation song used in conjunction with a public invitation. However, the song of response can serve other functions as well. For example, the song of response can be used to reinforce the message. A sermon on the transcendence and majesty of God could be followed by singing "Glorify Thy Name." A sermon on God as heavenly parent could be followed by singing "Children of the Heavenly Father." A sermon on social justice could be followed by "For the Healing of the Nations." Another option is to sing a general song of dedication such as "Here I Am, Lord," "Take My Life and Let It Be," or "The Gift of Love."

3. *Affirmation of faith.* After the song of response comes an affirmation of faith. Numerous options exist for this part of the worship service. Consider the following possibilities.

◇ *Biblical affirmations of faith.*

Leader: Let us now affirm our faith in God.

People: "The first [commandment] is, 'Hear, O Israel: the Lord our God, the Lord is one; you shall love the Lord your God with all your heart, and with all your soul, and with all your mind, and with all your strength.' The second is this, 'You shall love your neighbor as yourself.' There is no other commandment greater than these."
(Mark 12:29-31)

Leader: Who will separate us from the love of Christ? Will hardship, or distress, or persecution, or famine, or nakedness, or peril, or sword?

People: No, in all these things we are more than conquerors through him who loved us. For I am convinced that neither death, nor life, nor angels, nor rulers, nor things present, nor things to come, nor powers, nor height, nor depth, nor anything else in all creation, will be able to separate us from the love of God in Christ Jesus our Lord.

Leader: Thanks be to God!

People: Amen.   (Rom. 8:35, 37-39)

Leader: This is the good news which we have received, in which we stand, and by which we are saved:

People: Christ died for our sins, was buried, was raised on the third day, and appeared first to the women, then to Peter and the Twelve, and then to many faithful witnesses. We believe Jesus is the Christ, the Anointed One of God, the first-born of all creation, the firstborn from the dead, in whom all things hold together, in whom the fullness of God was pleased to dwell by the power of the Spirit. Christ is the head of the body, the church, and by the blood of the cross reconciles all things to God. Amen.
(1 Cor. 15:1-6 and Col. 1:15-20;
The United Methodist Hymnal, no. 888)

Leader: There is one God and there is one mediator, Christ Jesus, who came as a ransom for all, to whom we testify.

People: **This saying is sure and worthy of full acceptance; That Jesus Christ came into the world to save sinners, and was manifested in the flesh, vindicated in the Spirit, seen by angels, proclaimed among the nations, believed in throughout the world, taken up in glory. Great indeed is the mystery of the gospel. Amen.**

(1 Tim. 2:5-6, 1:15, 3:16;
The United Methodist Hymnal, no. 889)

◇ *Historic affirmations of faith.* The two great historic affirmations of faith of the church are the Nicene Creed and the Apostles' Creed.

The Nicene Creed

We believe in one God, the Father, the Almighty, maker of heaven and earth, of all that is, seen and unseen.

We believe in one Lord, Jesus Christ, the only Son of God, eternally begotten of the Father, God from God, Light from Light, true God from true God, begotten, not made, of one Being with the Father; through him all things were made. For us and for our salvation he came down from heaven, was incarnate of the Holy Spirit and the Virgin Mary and became truly human. For our sake he was crucified under Pontius Pilate; he suffered death and was buried. On the third day he rose again in accordance with the Scriptures; he ascended into heaven and is seated at the right hand of the Father. He will come again in glory to judge the living and the dead, and his kingdom will have no end.

We believe in the Holy Spirit, the Lord, the giver of life, who proceeds from the Father and the Son, who with the Father and the Son is worshiped and glorified, who has spoken through the prophets. We believe in the one holy catholic and apostolic church. We acknowledge one baptism for the forgiveness of sins. We look for the resurrection of the dead, and the life of the world to come. Amen.

The Apostles' Creed

I believe in God the Father Almighty, maker of heaven and earth;

And in Jesus Christ his only Son our Lord: who was conceived by the Holy Spirit, born of the Virgin Mary, suffered under Pontius Pilate, was crucified, dead, and buried; the third day he rose from the dead; he ascended into heaven, and sitteth at the right hand of God the Father Almighty; from thence he shall come to judge the quick and the dead.

I believe in the Holy Spirit, the holy catholic church, the communion of saints, the forgiveness of sins, the resurrection of the body, and the life everlasting. Amen.

◇ *Traditional affirmations of faith.*

We believe in God the Father, Creator, Ruler of all things, the source of all goodness, truth, and love.

We believe in Jesus Christ the Son, God manifest in the flesh, Redeemer and Lord, and ever-living head of the church.

We believe in the Holy Spirit, God ever-present, for guidance, comfort, and strength.

We affirm our faith in God and pledge anew to love the Lord our God with all our heart, soul, mind, and strength, and to love our neighbor as ourselves.

◇ *Contemporary affirmations of faith.*

We are not alone, we live in God's world. We believe in God: who has created and is creating, who has come in Jesus, the Word made flesh, to reconcile and make new, who works in us and others by the Spirit. We trust in God. We are called to be the church: to celebrate God's presence, to love and serve others, to seek justice and resist evil, to proclaim Jesus, crucified and risen, our judge and our hope. In life, in death, in life beyond death, God is with us. We are not alone. Thanks to be God. Amen.

(A Statement of Faith of the United Church of Canada, *The United Methodist Hymnal*, no. 883)

◇ *Musical affirmations of faith.* Although affirmations of faith are generally spoken, they can also be sung: "He Is Lord," "We Believe in One True God," "We Believe (in God the Father)," "We Believe in God Almighty," "What a Mighty God," "There Is One Lord," and "Fairest Lord Jesus." Consider Barry Liesch's poetic version of the Apostles' Creed that was designed to be sung to the familiar tune of "Glorious Things of Thee Are Spoken."

I believe in God the Father, Maker of the heaven and earth,
And in Jesus Christ, our Savior, God's own Son of matchless
   worth;
By the Holy Ghost conceived, Virgin Mary bore God's Son,
He, in whom I have believed, God Almighty, Three in One.

Suffered under Pontius Pilate, crucified for me He died.
Laid within the grave so silent, gates of Hell He opened wide,
And the stone-sealed tomb was empty, on the third day He arose,
Into heaven made His entry, Mighty Conqueror of His foes.

At God's right hand He is seated, till His coming, as He said,
Final judgment will be meted to the living and the dead;
I confess the Holy Spirit has been sent through Christ the Son,
To apply salvation's merit, God the Spirit—Three in One.

I believe that all believers form one body as a whole;
We are one throughout the ages, with the saints I lift my soul.
I believe sins are forgiven, that our bodies will be raised,
Everlasting life in heaven, Amen, let His name be praised!
> (Barry Liesch, *People in the Presence of God*
> [Grand Rapids: Zondervan, 1988], p. 108)

After the song of response and an affirmation of faith, the congregation is ready for a time of prayer, often called "Prayers of the People." However, if a baptism is scheduled, it is placed at this point in the service. If the church uses a historic baptism liturgy, then an affirmation of faith is not needed before the baptism, because the baptism liturgy includes a question-and-answer format of the Apostles' Creed.

4. *Baptism.* The celebration of the Sacrament of Holy Baptism is always a high moment for the congregation. The great liturgies of ancient baptism can hardly be improved upon. Other than the use of modern songs to begin or end a baptism service, consider using the ancient pattern. Historically, the liturgy of baptism includes

- ◇ introduction to the service
- ◇ presentation of candidates
- ◇ renunciation of sin and profession of faith
- ◇ thanksgiving over the water

83

◇ baptism with laying on of hands
◇ commendation and welcome

For information about baptism liturgies, explanations, and instructions, see appendix 2.

5. *Reaffirmation of baptism vows.* When celebrating baptism, some churches offer an opportunity for members of the congregation to reaffirm their baptism vows. The opportunity is announced the week before the baptism, and at the beginning of the baptism service. Although a simple ritual, it is profoundly meaningful for those who participate. After the baptism is over, people from the congregation are invited to come forward for the renewal of their baptism vows. As they walk to the baptismal font, the pastor dips her thumb into the water, places it on a member's forehead, makes the sign of the cross, and says, "Remember your baptism, and be a faithful follower of Jesus Christ." Singing songs of dedication during the renewal such as "He Is Lord," "I Surrender All," "Sanctuary," "Yes, Lord, Yes," and "Lord, I Want to Be a Christian" adds to this experience. More information about this powerful act of worship can be found in the baptism resources previously mentioned.

God's Call to Prayer

After affirming their faith, the congregation now observes a time of prayer (Prayers of the People). Prayer is obviously an essential part of the worship of God. Unfortunately, many churches tend to find themselves in a rut, using the same form of prayer Sunday after Sunday. However, a great variety of prayers exist that are appropriate for corporate worship services. Consider these possibilities:

1. *Begin with a spoken call to prayer.* Offer a spoken call to prayer before the prayer time begins. For example:

Leader:	In the midst of our praise,
People:	**be Thou our joy.**
Leader:	In the midst of our doubt,

People: **be Thou our faith.**
Leader: In the midst of our despair,
People: **be Thou our hope.**
Leader: In the midst of our fear,
People: **be Thou our strength.**
Leader: In the midst of our worship,
People: **be Thou present. Amen.**
             (*Be Thou Present: Prayers, Litanies, and Hymns*
                              for Christian Worship, p. 9)

Leader: Come to me, you who are tired, you who are burdened, come.
People: **We come with our hopes and our fears; we come as we are.**
Leader: I have loved you with an everlasting love. From your mother's womb, I have taken delight in you.
People: **We come in joy and in need; we come as we are.**
Leader: Today is the acceptable time, now is the hour of salvation. All who are burdened, come.
People: **Today is the acceptable time. Now is the hour of salvation. We come as we are.**
             (*More Than Words: Prayer and Ritual*
                        for Inclusive Communities, p. 54)

2. *Begin with a musical call to prayer.* From time to time, begin your prayer time by singing a musical call to prayer. Examples of songs include

◇ "Lord, Listen to Your Children Praying"
◇ "Sweet Hour of Prayer"
◇ "Surely the Presence of the Lord"
◇ "O Lord, Hear My Prayer"
◇ "Lead Me, Guide Me"
◇ "Near to the Heart of God"
◇ "Spirit of the Living God"
◇ "Turn Your Eyes Upon Jesus"

3. *Have one person lead the prayer.* One person, often the pastor, can lead a prayer on behalf of the congregation. In smaller churches, the entire congregation can share prayer concerns or celebrations before the prayer. The more specif-

ic the prayer, the stronger. For example, instead of praying for all those who are sick, offer specific names, such as "Sarah in Central Hospital who is recovering from surgery."

4. *Prepare a printed prayer.* Print a prayer in the church bulletin and pray in unison. This is especially appropriate in times of national or local tragedy. A printed prayer allows the congregation to share together, in one voice, their shared anger, loss, and need for God.

5. *Pray the Lord's Prayer.* Consider printing it in the bulletin, since everyone may not know this prayer by memory.

6. *Occasionally sing the Lord's Prayer.*

7. *Invite people to pray at the altar.* Extend an invitation for people to come to the altar and kneel in prayer. Many congregations do this weekly as part of the morning prayer.

8. *Lead a general guided prayer.* Invite people to offer prayers of (1) praise, (2) thanksgiving, (3) confession, (4) petition, and (5) surrender. After a brief introduction to each form of prayer, allow a time of silence for each person to pray.

9. *Lead a specific guided prayer.* Introduce more specific prayer concerns: Bill's upcoming surgery, the medical mission team as they prepare to go to the Philippines, people in Arkansas who lost their homes in a tornado, and so forth. After each concern, allow a time of silence for the congregation to pray.

10. *Have a "tag team" general prayer.* Ask four people (in advance) to come forward and lead the congregation in prayer. The first person offers a prayer of praise, the second a prayer of thanksgiving, the third a prayer of confession, and the fourth a prayer of petition.

11. *Have a "tag team" specific prayer.* Prior to worship, ask several people to briefly pray for specific needs in the congregation, community, or world.

12. *Pray in small groups.* Consider occasionally inviting the congregation to pray in small groups throughout the sanctuary. For example, during the time I pastored in Hawaii, Hurricane Iniki hit the Hawaiian Islands. Many people, especially on the island of Kauai, were hurt and

homeless. On the Sunday following the storm, in small groups throughout the congregation we prayed for the people in that crisis. It proved to be a powerful experience of worship. However, when choosing this prayer option, make sure that people are not forced to pray verbally, since some folks are terrified to pray aloud. Give them permission to pray silently.

13. *Offer special-needs prayers.* Invite people with special needs (for example, persons who have become unemployed or those who have recently lost loved ones) or people engaged in significant life transitions (recently engaged, married, divorced, retired, had first child, and so forth) to come forward for prayer. Lay hands on them and offer a prayer on their behalf.

Examples of these kinds of prayers can be found in *The United Methodist Book of Worship*, as well as other denominational prayer and worship books (see appendix 2).

14. *Offer special-occasion prayers.* For example, on the Sunday before the start of a new school year, pray the following prayer.

> Eternal God, we acknowledge that all wisdom comes from you. Thank you for the beginning of a new school year and for the opportunities of learning that it provides. We pray today for all teachers, staff, and students, especially those in this congregation. We ask you to bless them as they begin a new year of learning. Give them inquiring minds, receptive hearts, and creative energies. Grant them joy for teaching and excitement for learning. Help all of us to continually learn new truths and to grow in grace with you and others, through Jesus Christ our Lord. Amen.

15. *Observe a time of silent prayer.* Perhaps call it a "Discipline of Silence." Read Habakkuk 2:20 ("But the LORD is in his holy temple, let all the earth keep silence before him!") or Psalm 46:10 ("Be still, and know that I am God!"). Then invite people to observe a moment of silent prayer and meditation. Conclude with a brief closing prayer such as:

> Almighty and eternal God, ruler of all things in heaven and earth: Mercifully accept the prayers of your people, and

strengthen us to do your will; through Jesus Christ our Lord. Amen. *(Book of Common Prayer*, p. 394)

Eight of these brief closing prayers can be found in the *Book of Common Prayer* on pages 394-395. Another eight closing prayers can be found in the *Book of Common Worship*, pages 123-124. If a less formal style is preferred, end the prayer by saying, "Dear Lord, you have heard our prayers, both spoken and unspoken. We trust you with them, in the name of Jesus Christ our Lord. Amen."

16. *Lead a "bidding" prayer*. In a bidding prayer, the leader mentions a prayer concern, says "Lord, in your mercy," and the entire congregation responds "Hear our prayer." This process continues for every major concern. Here is an example of a formal bidding prayer used in liturgical churches:

Leader: Let us pray for the church and for the world.
Grant, Almighty God, that all who confess your name may be united in your truth, live together in your love, and reveal your glory in the world.
[*Silence*]
Lord, in your mercy
People: **Hear our prayer.**

Leader: Guide the people of this land, and of all the nations, in the ways of justice and peace; that we may honor one another and serve the common good.
[*Silence*]
Lord, in your mercy
People: **Hear our prayer.**

Leader: Give us all a reverence for the earth as your own creation, that we may use its resources rightly in the service of others and to your honor and glory.
[*Silence*]
Lord, in your mercy
People: **Hear our prayer.**

Leader: Bless all whose lives are closely linked with ours, and grant that we may serve Christ in them, and love one another as he loves us.

	[*Silence*] Lord, in your mercy
People:	**Hear our prayer.**

Leader:	Comfort and heal all those who suffer in body, mind, or spirit; give them courage and hope in their troubles, and bring them the joy of your salvation. [*Silence*] Lord, in your mercy
People:	**Hear our prayer.**

Leader:	We commend to your mercy all who have died, that your will for them may be fulfilled; and we pray that we may share with all your saints in your eternal kingdom. [*Silence*] Lord, in your mercy
People:	**Hear our prayer.**

[*The celebrant adds a concluding collect.*]

(*Book of Common Prayer*, pp. 388-389)

Although the above example is a formal liturgical bidding prayer, the same method can be used in a nonliturgical, more informal worship setting. The leader can mention various concerns of the congregation or ask worshipers to share their concerns. After each concern, the leader says, "Lord, in your mercy." The congregation responds, "Hear our prayer."

17. *Use prayer cards.* Place prayer cards, with space for writing prayer concerns, in the pew or the worship bulletins. During the announcements, ask people to fill the cards out. Immediately prior to the prayer time, have the ushers collect the cards and give them to the minister or worship leader. Read the prayer concerns aloud, and pray for them. This option is especially appropriate in larger churches, since it is not feasible for each person to share their concerns verbally.

18. *Share prayers of celebration.* Ask people to share joys and celebrations. After each one has, the leader says, "Lord, for your blessings." The congregation responds, "We give you thanks."

89

19. *Pray for healing and wholeness.* Perhaps once a month invite people to come to the altar area for prayers of wholeness and healing. Have the pastor or a lay minister place a small amount of olive oil on each person's forehead, making the sign of a cross, and say, "I anoint you with oil in the name of the Father, and of the Son, and of the Holy Spirit." Then lay hands on them and pray for wholeness (physical, mental, relational, or spiritual) in their life. This prayer can be general, such as "May the Holy Spirit bring wholeness into your life: mind, body, and soul; and may you be filled with the presence of Jesus Christ." Or, if the person shares his or her particular need, a more specific prayer can be offered.

Prayers for wholeness and healing should be carefully prepared. Although these prayers are not a substitute for medical or psychiatric treatment, they are part of a comprehensive approach to human wholeness, including the spiritual dimensions of healing. Before implementing prayers for wholeness and healing, see *The United Methodist Book of Worship* or the *Book of Common Worship* for an overview of healing prayers and services. Prayers for healing and wholeness can also be offered to people during Communion at a separate station. Consider asking lay worship leaders or ministers to lead this significant time of prayer.

20. *Lead a responsive reading prayer.* Here is a traditional example:

Leader:	Father, we pray for your Holy Catholic Church;
People:	**That we all may be one.**
Leader:	Grant that every member of the Church may truly and humbly serve you;
People:	**That your Name may be glorified by all people.**
Leader:	We pray for all bishops, priests, and deacons;
People:	**That they may be faithful ministers of your Word and Sacraments.**
Leader:	We pray for all who govern and hold authority in the nations of the world:
People:	**That there may be justice and peace on the earth.**
Leader:	Give us grace to do your will in all that we undertake;

People: **That our works may find favor in your sight.**
Leader: Have compassion on those who suffer from any grief or trouble;
People: **That they may be delivered from their distress.**
Leader: Give to the departed eternal rest;
People: **Let light perpetual shine upon them.**
Leader: We praise you for your saints who have entered into joy;
People: **May we also come to share in your heavenly kingdom.**
Leader: Let us pray for our own needs and those of others.
[Silence]

[The people may add their own petitions.]

Leader: Lord, hear the prayers of [your] people; and what we have asked faithfully, grant that we may obtain effectually, to the glory of [your] name; through Jesus Christ our Lord. Amen.
                        (*Book of Common Prayer,* pp. 387-388, 394)

Although this is a traditional, liturgical example of a responsive prayer litany, the same responsive reading method can be used in a more informal and contemporary setting.

21. *Pray prayers of dedication.* When members of your congregation embark upon a new ministry role, plan a prayer of dedication for them. For example, several men in my congregation participate in church-construction mission trips. The Sunday before they depart, we ask them to come to the chancel rail and kneel for prayer. Family, friends, and other interested persons are invited to lay hands on them while prayers are said on behalf of the men's mission effort. The same thing can be done for new teachers, choir members, and so forth. Excellent liturgies of dedication can be found in the "Commissioning for Lay Ministries in the Church" section of the *Book of Occasional Services: 1991* (New York: The Church Hymnal Corporation).

22. *Offer prayers of confession.* An ongoing debate exists concerning where the prayers of confession should be placed in public worship. Some worship leaders argue that it should come during the opening moments of the gathering, when

the congregation first comes into the presence of the Lord. Isaiah 6:1-8 is often used to illustrate this point. Other worship leaders advocate that the gathering is a festive time of joy, celebration, and praise, and should not be marred by a focus on human sin. Moreover, they suggest that awareness and confession of sin sometimes comes as a response to the service of the Word, and should therefore come afterward. I agree with this argument and generally place the prayer of confession (when we have one) after the service of the Word and during the response.

Some worship experts argue that weekly prayers of confession are inappropriate in Christian worship. James F. White, a liturgical scholar, asserts that a penitential focus in worship is simply a holdover from the Middle Ages. During the Middle Ages, says White, there was a "shift in emphasis away from an assembly gathered to rejoice in what God had done to an assembly of individuals met to bemoan their sin before the Almighty." This medieval penitential approach was continued by Reformers like Calvin and, unfortunately, is still prevalent among many Protestant churches today. According to White, prayers of confession are unnecessary in most worship services. Instead, penitential rites should be occasional acts only, particularly during the seasons of Advent and Lent. He also argues that the prayer of confession, when it is added at all, should come after the service of the Word and not during the gathering (*Introduction to Christian Worship*, pp. 148, 150, 161).

I concur with White; I see no good reason to have a prayer of confession every Sunday. Christians gather for worship to celebrate the mighty acts of God, not to focus on their unworthiness. Therefore my congregation offers prayers of confession regularly during Lent and Advent, and only occasionally during the rest of the year.

Begin the prayer of confession with a brief call to confession, such as "Let us confess our sins against God and our neighbor." After a moment of silence, proceed with the prayer. Here is an ancient prayer of confession and assurance of pardon:

Leader: Have mercy on me, O God, according to your steadfast love; according to your abundant mercy blot out my transgressions.

People: **Wash me thoroughly from my iniquity, and cleanse me from my sin.**

Leader: For I know my transgressions, and my sin is ever before me.

People: **Against you, you alone, have I sinned, and done what is evil in your sight, so that you are justified in your sentence and blameless when you pass judgment.**

Leader: Purge me with hyssop, and I shall be clean;

People: **wash me, and I shall be whiter than snow.**

Leader: Hide your face from my sins, and blot out all my iniquities.

People: **Create in me a clean heart, O God, and put a new and right spirit within me.**

Leader: Do not cast me away from your presence, and do not take your holy spirit from me.

People: **Restore to me the joy of your salvation, and sustain in me a willing spirit.**

Leader: Then I will teach transgressors your ways,

People: **and sinners will return to you.**

[*Silence*]

Leader: If we confess our sins, he who is faithful and just will forgive us our sins and cleanse us from all unrighteousness.

People: **Thanks be to God!**

(Ps. 51:1-4, 7, 9-13; 1 John 1:9)

Here is a traditional prayer of confession and assurance of pardon:

Leader: Let us confess our sins against God and our neighbor.

People: **Most merciful God, we confess that we have sinned against you in thought, word, and deed, by what we have done, and by what we have left undone. We have not loved you with our whole heart; we have not loved our neighbors as ourselves. We are truly sorry and we humbly repent. For the sake of your Son Jesus Christ, have mercy on us and forgive us, that we may delight in your will, and walk in your ways, to the glory of your name. Amen.**

Leader: [*All pray in silence*]

Leader: Almighty God have mercy on you, forgive all your sins through our Lord Jesus Christ, strengthen you in all goodness, and by the power of the Holy Spirit keep you in eternal life.

People: **Amen.**

            (*The United Methodist Hymnal*, no. 890)

A contemporary prayer of confession:

Leader: Lord, we confess our day to day failure to be truly human.

People: **Lord, we confess to you.**

Leader: Lord, we confess that we often fail to love with all we have and are, often because we do not fully understand what loving means, often because we are afraid of risking ourselves.

People: **Lord, we confess to you.**

Leader: Lord, we cut ourselves off from each other and we erect barriers of division.

People: **Lord, we confess to you.**

Leader: Lord, we confess that by silence and ill-considered word

People: **we have built up walls of prejudice.**

Leader: Lord, we confess that by selfishness and lack of sympathy

People: **we have stifled generosity and left little time for others.**

Leader: Holy Spirit, speak to us. Help us listen to your word of forgiveness, for we are very deaf. Come, fill this moment and free us from sin.

            (*The United Methodist Hymnal*, no. 893)

The above suggestions do not exhaust the possibilities for prayer during a Sunday morning worship service. Prayers of confession can be found in virtually all prayer and worship books. Additional forms of historic Prayers of the People can be found in the *Book of Common Prayer* and the *Book of Common Worship*.

God's Call to Stewardship

The offering follows the Prayers of the People. Although brief, the offering is an important part of worship. In Psalm

96:8 we read, "Ascribe to the LORD the glory due his name, bring an offering, and come into his courts." Consider the following suggestions for enhancing the offering.

1. *Make the offering tangible.* Many people have no idea what happens to the money that is placed in the offering plate. Occasionally, highlight specific examples of how the money is used (for example, the money helps support the local food bank; paid for the recent youth mission trip to New Mexico; supports cancer research at Children's Hospital, and so forth). Short stories about where the money goes makes the offering tangible and encourages people to give.

2. *Read a brief Scripture passage before receiving the offering.* For example:

The earth is the Lord's and all that is in it, the world, and those who live in it.

(Ps. 24:1)

Freely ye have received, freely give.

(Matt. 10:8*b* KJV)

Each of you must give as you have made up your mind, not reluctantly or under compulsion, for God loves a cheerful giver.

(2 Cor. 9:7)

Do not neglect to do good and to share what you have, for such sacrifices are pleasing to God.

(Heb. 13:16)

Remembering the words of the Lord Jesus, for he himself said, "It is more blessed to give than to receive."

(Acts 20:35*b*)

Ascribe to the LORD the glory due his name, bring an offering, and come into his courts.

(Ps. 96:8)

3. *Pray an offering prayer.* It could be as simple as "Dear Lord, we bring our tithes and offerings as an act of love and worship. Dedicate the giver and gift for service in your king-

dom; in the name of him who gave his all for us. Amen."

Although a minister, lay worship leader, or usher usually offers the offertory prayer, occasionally print the prayer in the bulletin and ask the congregation to pray in unison.

4. *Use music to enhance the offering.* Appropriate solos, anthems, hymns and choruses before, during, and after the offering can help enhance its meaning. Although most churches play instrumental music during the offering, choral anthems, solos, and congregational singing are also highly effective.

God's Call to Community

Early in its history, the church incorporated the "passing of the peace" into its experience of worship. The minister said to the congregation, "The peace of Christ be with you." The congregation responded, "And also with you." At that point the ritual was repeated, along with physical touch (in the ancient world a kiss would have been customary), by individual members of the congregation. In small congregations, the peace was passed with everyone. In large churches, the peace was passed to those standing nearby. This beautiful expression of Christian community has solid biblical roots. In Romans 16, Paul spoke about greeting the saints. He said in verse 16, "Greet one another with a holy kiss." In 1 Peter 5:14 we read, "Greet one another with a kiss of love." In 1 Corinthians 16:20, Paul said, "Greet one another with a holy kiss." He said the same in 2 Corinthians 13:12. In 1 Thessalonians 5:26, we read, "Greet all the brothers and sisters with a holy kiss."

This greeting, or passing of the peace, serves as a strong symbol of Christian love and community. The exchange of the peace occurs with a handshake, a hug, or a kiss. Historically, the passing of the peace has been placed after the offering and before the observance of the Lord's Supper. It reminds worshipers that they come to the Table not only as individuals, but as a community of faith.

However, the passing of the peace can also be placed during the opening movement—"We Gather to Worship God"—after the opening song, and before the opening prayer.

Introduce the passing of the peace with one of these greetings:

Leader: The peace of Christ be with you.
People: **And also with you.**

Leader: [*Easter season*] The peace of the risen Christ be with you.
People: **And also with you.**

Leader: The peace of the Lord be always with you.
People: **And also with you.**

Leader: As our Lord said to his disciples, "Peace be with you."
People: **And also with you.**

The most effective way to bring closure to the passing of the peace is with music. One option is to end the passing of the peace with a brief praise chorus. The choir begins the chorus, and the people immediately join in. The words to the chorus are printed in the bulletin.

Chapter 5

We Celebrate at the Table of God

The most serious deficiency in Protestant worship today, both in mainline and evangelical churches, is a lack of transcendence. Returning the Sacrament of Holy Eucharist to the center of Christian worship offers the most promising solution to this problem. When properly celebrated, the Lord's Supper highlights the mighty acts of God—past, present, and future—and celebrates the presence of the resurrected Christ in our midst through the action of the Holy Spirit. As a result, the worshiping community experiences the majesty and mystery of God's presence, returning an atmosphere of transcendence to worship, and renewing not only the worship of God but also the people of God.

The Centrality of Holy Communion

For fifteen hundred years the church celebrated the Lord's Supper weekly as the climax of Christian worship. However, three historical factors diminished the centrality of the Lord's Supper in most Protestant churches:

◇ the Reformation of the sixteenth century that emphasized *Word over Sacrament*
◇ the Enlightenment of the eighteenth century that emphasized *mind over mystery*

◇ the Camp Meeting movement of the nineteenth century that emphasized *evangelism over worship*

At present, a significant Eucharistic renewal is occurring in almost all denominations, and the Lord's Supper is once again becoming a vital element of Christian worship. Churches that historically observed Eucharist only once a quarter are moving to monthly observance, while churches that observed Eucharist monthly are moving toward weekly observance. After several centuries of decline, the Lord's Supper is once again becoming a central act of worship.

God's Love Made Visible

At least two great affirmations can be made about the Sacrament of the Lord's Supper. First, through the Eucharist, God is engaged in self-giving. Second, God's love is made visible through the physical elements, actions, and words of Holy Communion. Sacramental theology understands that human beings need concrete, visible, and outward signs of God's love. Humans are not pure spirit, but flesh and blood. Since our lives are intimately connected with matter, we need material aids to help us worship. In this way, Christianity is a "materialistic" religion. Indeed, our sacramental heritage points to the fact that we are a religion of the incarnation. God, in order to reveal love to humanity, became flesh and blood. And God continues to express love toward us through material objects like the water of baptism and the bread and wine of Holy Communion.

Along with the water of baptism and the oil of anointing, the early church used the physical elements of bread and wine to express significant spiritual truth. This practice of using physical objects to express spiritual truth was not new for them and was deeply rooted in their Jewish heritage. In the Old Testament, God often used physical objects to reveal God's self. Examples include the burning bush, the pillar of fire by night, the cloud by day, manna, and most significant—the Passover meal. The early church understood that

God often used material objects as channels of spiritual truth, and the church continued that tradition through the Sacraments of Baptism and the Lord's Supper.

New Testament Images of the Lord's Supper

A careful study of the New Testament reveals numerous images of the Lord's Supper. As you plan for Communion services, emphasize each of them over time.

1. *Thanksgiving* (Matt. 26:26; Mark 14:22; Luke 22:17). The Gospel accounts of the Lord's Supper all record that Jesus gave thanks before serving the meal. In Acts 2:46 we learn that the early Christians broke bread with "glad and generous" hearts. The early church called the Lord's Supper "Eucharist," which means to give thanks. In the *Didache*, an early discipleship manual, instructions for taking the Lord's Supper include giving thanks to God. It is important for today's worshipers to reclaim this element of joyful thanksgiving in our observance of Holy Communion. Rather than a somber and penitential attitude, Christians should come to the table with exhilarating joy, exuberant celebration, and joyful thanksgiving.

2. *Remembrance* (1 Cor. 11:24; Luke 22:19). When our Lord instituted the Lord's Supper, he commanded that we do so "in remembrance" of him. In the Eucharist we remember the life, death, and resurrection of Christ. However, this remembrance is more than mere memory; it is a reliving of the events of the Gospels. This happens most powerfully in the prayer of Great Thanksgiving, which recalls God's redemptive acts in Jesus Christ.

3. *Community* (1 Cor. 10:16-17). In this text, Paul says, "Because there is one bread, we who are many are one body, for we all partake of the one bread" (v. 17). The Lord's Supper is not an individual act, but a community event. It reminds us that we are part of a family, that we gather around the Father's table as brothers and sisters united in Christ.

4. *Sacrifice* (Matt. 26:28, Luke 22:20, 1 Cor. 11:25-26). The Lord's Supper is a vivid reminder that Christ's body was

101

broken and that his blood was shed on our behalf. The Supper not only symbolizes Christ's sacrificial death, but reminds us of his entire life of service and sacrifice for others. However, rather than somber remembrance, Christ's sacrifice on the cross should evoke joyful and celebrative praise, as seen in the book of Revelation:

> Then I looked, and I heard the voice of many angels surrounding the throne and the living creatures and the elders; they numbered myriads of myriads and thousands of thousands, singing with full voice, "Worthy is the Lamb that was slaughtered to receive power and wealth and wisdom and might and honor and glory and blessing!" Then I heard every creature in heaven and on earth and under the earth and in the sea, and all that is in them, singing, "To the one seated on the throne and to the Lamb be blessing and honor and glory and might forever and ever!" And the four living creatures said, "Amen!" And the elders fell down and worshiped.
>
> (Rev. 5:11-14)

5. *Christ's presence* (Matt. 26:26, 28; Mark 14:22-24; Luke 22:19; 1 Cor. 11:24-25). The early church did not debate the theological nuances of the actual presence of Christ in the Lord's Supper. They simply affirmed, celebrated, and enjoyed Christ's presence with them in the breaking of the bread and the drinking of the wine. Regardless of our particular denominational theology, we, like the early Christians, can join in joyful celebration of Christ's presence with us as we partake of the holy meal.

6. *Foretaste of the coming kingdom of God* (Luke 22:16; Matt. 26:29; Mark 14:25; 1 Cor. 11:26). The Lord's Supper also has an eschatological meaning. It is a foretaste of the future consummation and fullness of God's coming kingdom. When we observe Communion, we anticipate the day when believers from every age will finally be home, gathered around God's table, singing and feasting and celebrating the final triumph of Jesus Christ and his holy bride, the church.

7. *Action of the Holy Spirit*. Although no direct New Testament references are made relating the Holy Spirit to the Sacrament of the Lord's Supper, the early church saw a clear

relationship between them. For example, in the writing of Hippolytus, around 115 A.D., we find liturgical records where the Lord's Supper is connected with the action of the Holy Spirit. Indeed, every Eucharist liturgy throughout the history of the church makes this important connection between the Lord's Supper and the activity of the Holy Spirit.

A Biblical-Historical Pattern of Holy Communion

The early church soon developed a fourfold pattern for observing Eucharist. A close examination of the accounts of the Lord's Supper reveal this fourfold pattern. Mark 14:22 records, "While they were eating, he took a loaf of bread, and after blessing it he broke it, gave it to them, and said, 'Take; this is my body.' " In Luke's account of the Emmaus experience, we read, "When he was at the table with them, he took bread, blessed and broke it, and gave it to them" (Luke 24:30). The same pattern can be found in numerous miracle feeding stories, such as Mark 6:41: "Taking the five loaves and the two fish, he looked up to heaven, and blessed and broke the loaves, and gave them to his disciples to set before the people." The four-fold pattern is obvious in these and other texts:

◇ he *took*
◇ he *blessed*
◇ he *broke*
◇ he *gave*

These four movements—taking, blessing, breaking, and giving—soon became the formal liturgy of the Table.

1. *He took.* First, Jesus took the bread and wine in his hands. In the early church, members actually brought bread and wine for the Lord's Supper as part of their offering. After the service of the Word, they brought their gifts of bread and wine to the Lord's Supper table. Many churches continue this practice by asking individuals or families to bake bread for

the Lord's Supper and bring it to the table as the Supper begins. If the elements are already on the Lord's Supper table, the minister can lift them up for the congregation to see; or, if the elements are covered, the covering can be removed, symbolizing that the observance of the Supper is about to begin. The singing of a hymn or chorus such as "Open Our Eyes, Lord" or "Surely the Presence of the Lord" adds much to this part of the service.

2. *He blessed.* Next, Jesus blessed the elements. Early on, the church developed a special prayer for the Lord's Supper, called the "Great Thanksgiving." This prayer celebrates God's acts in history, especially God's redemptive activity in the life, death, and resurrection of Christ. Using the Great Thanksgiving significantly enhances the meaning of the Lord's Supper. Although the following example appears in *The United Methodist Book of Worship*, it is similar to the Great Thanksgiving in all Christian traditions.

The pastor, standing if possible behind the Lord's Table, facing the people from this time through Breaking the Bread, takes the bread and cup; and the bread and wine are prepared for the meal.

Leader:	The Lord be with you.
People:	**And also with you.**
Leader:	Lift up your hearts.

The pastor may lift hands and keep them raised.

People:	**We lift them up to the Lord.**
Leader:	Let us give thanks to the Lord our God.
People:	**It is right to give our thanks and praise.**

Leader:	It is right, and a good and joyful thing, always and everywhere to give thanks to you, Father Almighty, creator of heaven and earth. You formed us in your image and breathed into us the breath of life. When we turned away, and our love failed, your love remained steadfast. You delivered us from captivity, made covenant to be our sovereign God, and spoke to us through your prophets. And so, with your people on earth and all the company of heaven we praise your name and join their unending hymn:

The pastor may lower hands.

People: Holy, holy, holy Lord, God of power and might, heaven and earth are full of your glory. Hosanna in the highest. Blessed is he who comes in the name of the Lord. Hosanna in the highest.

The pastor may raise hands.

Leader: Holy are you, and blessed is your Son Jesus Christ. Your Spirit anointed him to preach good news to the poor, to proclaim release to the captives and recovering of sight to the blind, to set at liberty those who are oppressed, and to announce that the time had come when you would save your people.

He healed the sick, fed the hungry, and ate with sinners. By the baptism of his suffering, death, and resurrection you gave birth to your church, delivered us from slavery to sin and death, and made with us a new covenant by water and the Spirit.

When the Lord Jesus ascended, he promised to be with us always, in the power of your Word and Holy Spirit.

The pastor may hold hands, palms down, over the bread, or touch the bread, or lift the bread.

Leader: On the night in which he gave himself up for us, he took bread, gave thanks to you, broke the bread, gave it to his disciples, and said: "Take, eat; this is my body which is given for you. Do this in remembrance of me."

The pastor may hold hands, palms down, over the cup, or touch the cup, or lift the cup.

Leader: When the supper was over, he took the cup, gave thanks to you, gave it to his disciples, and said: "Drink from this, all of you; this is my blood of the new covenant, poured out for you and for many for the forgiveness of sins. Do this, as often as you drink it, in remembrance of me."

The pastor may raise hands.

Leader: And so, in remembrance of these your mighty acts in Jesus Christ, we offer ourselves in praise and thanksgiving as a holy and living sacrifice, in union with Christ's offering for us, as we proclaim the mystery of faith.

People: **Christ has died; Christ is risen; Christ will come again.**

The pastor may hold hands, palms down, over the bread and cup.

Leader: Pour out your Holy Spirit on us gathered here, and on these gifts of bread and wine. Make them be for us the body and blood of Christ, that we may be for the world the body of Christ, redeemed by his blood.

Pastor may raise hands.

Leader: By your Spirit make us one with Christ, and one with each other, and one in ministry to all the world, until Christ comes in final victory and we feast at his heavenly banquet. Through your Son Jesus Christ, with the Holy Spirit in your holy church, all honor and glory is yours, almighty Father, now and for ever.

People: **Amen.**

Leader: And now, with the confidence of children of God, let us pray:

The pastor may raise hands.
All pray the Lord's Prayer.
              (*The United Methodist Book of Worship*, pp. 36-38)

Although a formal Great Thanksgiving prayer is associated with liturgical churches, a growing number of contemporary and charismatic churches are including this prayer in their Communion services. Many find it adds spiritual depth to their observance of the Lord's Supper, and connects them to a long heritage of Christian worship. Blending this ancient prayer with modern songs has a powerful impact on worshipers. The prayer can easily be adapted for any context. For example, less formal language can be used, and the prayer can be simplified and/or shortened. However, the basic pattern should remain:

◇ an invitation to give thanks to God
◇ thanksgiving for God's creation and providence in history
◇ thanksgiving for the work of Christ
◇ the words of institution (1 Cor. 11:23b-26)
◇ prayer for the Spirit to come upon us and upon the elements
◇ the Lord's Prayer

If congregational responses are used, either print the entire prayer in the bulletin (perhaps as an insert) or simply print the congregational responses, with a brief introduction so that people will know when to respond. For example:

Leader:	The Lord be with you.
People:	**And also with you.**
Leader:	Lift up your hearts.
People:	**We lift them up to the Lord.**
Leader:	Let us give thanks to the Lord our God.
People:	**It is right to give our thanks and praise.**
Leader:	We praise your name and join their unending hymn:
People:	**Holy, holy, holy Lord, God of power and might, heaven and earth are full of your glory. Hosanna in the highest. Blessed is he who comes in the name of the Lord. Hosanna in the highest.**
Leader:	As we proclaim the mystery of faith:
People:	**Christ has died; Christ is risen; Christ will come again.**

(adapted from *The United Methodist Hymnal*, pp. 9-10)

Many variations of the Great Thanksgiving prayer can be found in the *Book of Common Prayer*, the *Book of Common Worship*, and other denominational books of worship (see appendix 2). In addition, musical variations are also available.

3. *He broke.* After the blessing, Jesus broke the bread. At the appropriate moment in the Lord's Supper, the minister holds up a piece of bread and breaks it. This breaking, called the fraction, can be done in silence or accompanied by words. For example: "Because there is one loaf, we, who are many, are one body, for we all partake of the one loaf. The bread that we break is a sharing in the body of Christ." Or, "The gifts of God for the people of God."

4. *He gave.* Finally, Jesus gave the bread and wine to his disciples. At this point in the service, the minister invites the people to partake of the elements with words such as "Come, brothers and sisters in Christ, let us partake. God has prepared for us a great feast. Let us receive this holy meal with glad and generous hearts."

Enriching the Lord's Supper

When preparing to observe the Lord's Supper, consider the following suggestions.

1. *Observe the Lord's Supper more often.* Most objections to observing more frequent Eucharist can be overcome. Many people dislike the somber atmosphere of most Communion services. However, funeral-like Communion services, with certain exceptions such as Passion Sunday or Holy Thursday, are inappropriate anyway. The Lord's Supper should be a joyful celebration.

Some people argue that frequent observance will make Communion less special, when, in fact, the exact opposite is true. Churches that celebrate Eucharist weekly invest enormous meaning into its observance. The argument that frequent Communion diminishes its special meaning just does not hold water. Should this same argument be applied to receiving a hug or a kiss? Should married couples have physical intimacy only once a quarter in order to keep it more special? Of course not!

Perhaps the strongest argument against frequent Eucharist is that it takes too much time. This too can be overcome by better planning of worship services, shortening sermons, and increasing the speed of Communion distribution. Multiple stations could be established for the congregation to receive the elements. The ushers could distribute from both the front and the rear of the sanctuary at the same time, if the congregation receives Communion while seated. Another alternative is to purchase Communion plates that hold both cups and bread, so as to limit the number of times the elements must be passed. Other objections can be overcome if the congregation is taught about the importance of Eucharist. If the church is currently observing quarterly Eucharist, move to monthly observance. If the church is observing monthly Eucharist, increase it to twice per month, perhaps on the first and third Sundays of the month. And, if the church is observing Eucharist twice per month, move toward weekly observance. Weekly observance of Word and Table has been the norm for most of our Christian history and, in my opinion, should ultimately be the goal of every worship leader.

2. *Have the congregation come forward to receive the Lord's Supper.* The impact of the Eucharist is far greater when people come forward to receive rather than remain in their pew. Of course, those unable to come to the altar are served at their seat.

3. *Invite the congregation to sing hymns and choruses during the distribution of the elements.* Singing songs during the distribution, both traditional and contemporary, enhances the meaning of the Lord's Supper. This is an important key if the congregation is to experience joyful celebrations of Holy Communion. A number of songs have been written specifically for the Lord's Supper. Examples include

- ◇ "Come, Sinners, to the Gospel Feast"
- ◇ "Let Us Break Bread Together"
- ◇ "One Bread, One Body"
- ◇ "Come, Let Us Eat"
- ◇ "Fill My Cup, Lord"
- ◇ "Broken for Me"
- ◇ "Eat This Bread"
- ◇ "Come, Share the Lord"

Other hymns and choruses, while not specifically written for Communion, are also good choices:

- ◇ "Love Divine, All Loves Excelling"
- ◇ "Sing Alleluia to the Lord"
- ◇ "Lamb of God"
- ◇ "I Will Change Your Name"
- ◇ "Let All Mortal Flesh Keep Silence"
- ◇ "O Sacred Head, Now Wounded"
- ◇ "When I Survey the Wondrous Cross"

Actually, any song that celebrates God's love and redemption, or offers praise and worship to the Almighty, is appropriate. Also, consider selecting songs that fit with the theme of the worship service or sermon. Simply list the song numbers in the bulletin, print the words as a bulletin insert, or place them on an overhead projector.

4. *Use real bread, and use larger pieces.* The hard and tiny chips of bread that are often used for the Lord's Supper do not lend themselves to a rich Communion experience. Consider purchasing larger Communion wafers, asking a member of the congregation to bake a loaf of bread, or using pita bread.

5. *Extend the Supper to those unable to attend.* In some of the earliest nonbiblical records of the early church, references are made to taking the Lord's Supper to those unable to attend public worship services. Many congregations take Communion to the shut-in members on the first Sunday of each month. If so, the following could be used to conclude Communion:

Before we leave the Table of the Lord, let us remember those in our church family who would like to be here today to receive Communion but who cannot. We share this holy meal with them and remember them as being a part of our church family. The Sacrament of Holy Eucharist will be taken today to the following persons: (each name is called). Let us pray.

Eternal God, you have bound us together as the body of Christ. We remember today those who will share with us in the holy sacrament. According to their particular needs, and by the power of your Spirit, minister to their needs. Strengthen them spiritually and physically, and enable them to sense our love and concern for them, through Jesus Christ, the Host of our Table. Amen. (adapted from *Eucharist: Christ's Feast with the Church,* pp. 156-157)

The following liturgy can be used for home visits. A different Scripture reading is read each month.

Scripture Reading

Who will separate us from the love of Christ? Will hardship, or distress, or persecution, or famine, or nakedness, or peril, or sword? No, in all these things we are more than conquerors through him who loved us. For I am convinced that neither death, nor life, nor angels, nor rulers, nor things present, nor things to come, nor powers, nor height, nor depth, nor anything else in all creation, will be able to separate us from the love of God in Christ Jesus our Lord." (Rom. 8:35, 37-39)

Invitation

Christ our Lord invites to his Table all who love him. Let us draw near with faith and prepare to receive this Holy Sacrament.

The Lord's Prayer

Let us pray as Jesus taught us, saying, "Our Father, who art in heaven, hallowed be thy name; thy kingdom come, thy will be done on earth as it is in heaven. Give us this day our daily bread. And forgive us our trespasses, as we forgive those who trespass against us. And lead us not into temptation, but deliver us from evil. For thine is the kingdom, and the power, and the glory, forever. Amen."

Words of Institution

On the night in which Jesus gave himself up for us he took bread, gave thanks, broke the bread, gave it to his disciples, and said: "Take, eat; this is my body, which is given for you. Do this in remembrance of me." When the supper was over, he took the cup, gave thanks, gave it to his disciples, and said: "Drink from this, all of you; this is my blood of the new covenant, poured out for you and for many for the forgiveness of sins. Do this, as often as you drink it, in remembrance of me."

111

Giving the Bread and Cup

_____ (name) the body of Christ, given for you. Amen.
_____ (name) the blood of Christ, given for you. Amen.

Prayer

Let us pray: "Loving God, we thank you that you have fed us in this Sacrament, united us with Christ, and given us a foretaste of your heavenly banquet in your eternal kingdom." [*Conclude with a specific prayer for the individual.*]

(*Book of Common Worship*, p. 76)

Blessing

The grace of the Lord Jesus Christ, and the love of God, and the communion of the Holy Spirit be with you [all]. Amen.

6. *Teach the congregation about the Sacrament of Holy Communion.* A teaching guide can be used in an adult Sunday school class to help the congregation learn more about the significance of the sacraments. As a way of introducing the material, affirm that the Sacrament of Holy Communion (and Baptism) involves (1) God's self-giving and (2) God's love made visible. Next, use the acrostic "SUPPER" to review the major New Testament images of the Lord's Supper:

Sacrifice of Christ
Unity of believers
Presence of Christ
Promise of coming kingdom
Eucharist (to give thanks)
Remembrance of the gospel

Conclude the class by celebrating the Lord's Supper. The listening guide for class members appears on page 114:

When Communion Is Not Celebrated

Many Protestant churches do not observe weekly Communion. On the Sundays when Communion is not observed, there are two options related to the order of the service.

1. Move directly from the third movement of worship, "We Respond to the Call of God," to the fifth movement, "We Depart to Serve God."

2. Substitute "We Offer Thanks to God" for "We Celebrate at the Table of God." During this alternative movement of worship, the congregation is led in a prayer of thanksgiving before the departure. It is appropriate to lead the prayer from behind the Lord's Supper table, as is done with the Great Thanksgiving. Although the prayer is not as extensive as the Great Thanksgiving, it has enough similarities to remind the congregation of Communion and to make them hungry for their next opportunity to gather around the Table. An example follows:

We Offer Thanks to God

Leader:	Let us give thanks to the Lord our God.
People:	**It is right to give our thanks and praise.**
Leader:	Eternal God, creator of the world and giver of all good, we thank you for the earth, our home, and for the gift of life. We praise you for your love in Jesus Christ, who came to heal this broken world, who died rejected on the cross and rose triumphant from the dead. Because he lives, we live to praise you, our God forever.
People:	**Gracious God, who called us from death to life, we give ourselves to you; and with the church through all ages we thank you for your saving love in Jesus Christ our Lord. Amen.**

(Book of Common Worship, p. 80)

Many additional examples of the prayer of thanksgiving can be found in the *Book of Common Worship.*

After the prayer of thanksgiving, move to the final movement of worship—"We Depart to Serve God."

The Sacrament of Holy Communion

1. God's _____ _____
2. God's love _____ _____

Biblical Images of the Lord's Supper

S_____

"This is my blood . . . which is poured out for many for the forgiveness of sins" (Matt. 26:28).

"By the baptism of his suffering, death, and resurrection you gave birth to your church . . ." (from the Great Thanksgiving prayer).

U_____

"Because there is one bread, we who are many are one body, for we all partake of the one bread" (1 Cor. 10:17).

"By your Spirit make us one with Christ, and one with each other, and one in ministry to all the world . . ." (Great Thanksgiving).

P_____

"This is my body . . . my blood . . ." (Matt. 26:26, 28).

"Pour out your Holy Spirit on . . . these gifts of bread and wine. Make them be for us the body and blood of Christ . . ." (Great Thanksgiving).

P_____

"I will never again drink of this fruit of the vine until that day when I drink it new with you in my Father's kingdom" (Matt. 26:29).

"Until Christ comes in final victory, and we feast at his heavenly banquet" (Great Thanksgiving).

E_____

"Then he took a cup, and after giving thanks. . . . Then he took a loaf of bread, and when he had given thanks . . ." (Luke 22:17, 19).

"It is right, and a good and joyful thing, always and everywhere to give thanks to you, Father Almighty" (Great Thanksgiving).

R_____

"Do this in remembrance of me" (Luke 22:19).

"And so, in remembrance of these your mighty acts in Jesus Christ . . ." (Great Thanksgiving).

Chapter 6

We Depart to
Serve God

Hoyt Hickman tells the story about a Quaker who
invited his friend to join him for silent worship at a
Quaker meetinghouse. Not knowing the customs of
the Quakers, the friend was confused when he saw the congregation sitting in silence. After several minutes of silence,
he whispered to his host, "When does the service begin?" His
friend replied, "When the meeting has ended" (*Worshiping
with United Methodists* [Nashville: Abingdon Press, 1996],
p. 77).

After the congregation has gathered to worship God, lis-
tened to the Word of God, responded to the call of God, and
celebrated at the Table of God, they are ready for the final
movement of worship—departure to serve God. This is a
short yet important movement of worship. The departure
brings closure to the worship service and sends the congregation forth to serve God in the world. The departure usually includes the following components:

◇ post-Communion prayer
◇ pastoral benediction
◇ closing song
◇ words of dismissal

Post-Communion Prayer

Although this prayer can be included in the fourth movement ("We Celebrate at the Table of God"), it is placed here

115

because it concludes by asking God to send us into the world as servants of Christ. Examples of this closing prayer are the following:

> Eternal God, we give you thanks for this holy mystery in which you have given yourself to us. Grant that we may go into the world in the strength of your Spirit, to give ourselves for others, in the name of Jesus Christ our Lord. Amen.
> *(The United Methodist Hymnal*, p. 11)

> Eternal God, heavenly Father, you have graciously accepted us as living members of your Son our Savior Jesus Christ, and you have fed us with spiritual food in the Sacrament of his Body and Blood. Send us now into the world in peace, and grant us strength and courage to love and serve you with gladness and singleness of heart; through Christ our Lord. Amen.
> *(Book of Common Prayer*, p. 365)

> Loving God, we thank you that you have fed us in this Sacrament, united us with Christ, and given us a foretaste of the heavenly banquet in your eternal kingdom. Send us out in the power of your Spirit to live and work to your praise and glory, for the sake of Jesus Christ our Lord. Amen.
> *(Book of Common Worship*, p. 76)

Other examples can be found in the *Book of Worship: United Church of Christ* and *Thankful Praise: A Resource for Christian Worship*, the book of worship for the Christian Church (Disciples of Christ) (see appendix 2).

Although this prayer can be led by the pastor or another worship leader, consider printing it in the bulletin so that the entire congregation can pray together. On those Sundays when Communion is not served, this closing prayer can easily be adapted by simply deleting the references to the Lord's Supper. Instead, substitute words of thanks for the worship just experienced. For example:

> Eternal God, we give you thanks for visiting us in this hour of worship. Grant that we may go into the world in the strength of your Spirit, to give ourselves for others, in the name of Jesus Christ our Lord. Amen.
> (adapted from *The United Methodist Hymnal*, p. 11)

Pastoral Benediction

Immediately following the post-Communion prayer is the pastoral benediction. Traditionally, the pastor raises his or her right hand and announces the benediction while looking at the congregation. The benediction can be a blessing, a charge, or a combination of both. It can be spoken by the pastor only, or done as a responsive reading.

The grace of the Lord Jesus Christ, the love of God, and the communion of the Holy Spirit be with all of you.

(2 Cor. 13:13)

And the peace of God, which surpasses all understanding, will guard your hearts and your minds in Christ Jesus.

(Phil. 4:7)

The LORD bless you and keep you; the LORD make his face to shine upon you, and be gracious to you; the LORD lift up his countenance upon you, and give you peace.

(Num. 6:24-26)

Now may the God of peace, who brought back from the dead our Lord Jesus, the great shepherd of the sheep, by the blood of the eternal covenant, make you complete in everything good so that you may do his will, working among us that which is pleasing in his sight, through Jesus Christ, to whom be the glory forever and ever. Amen.

(Heb. 13:20-21)

May the God of hope fill you with all joy and peace in believing, so that you may abound in hope by the power of the Holy Spirit.

(Rom 15:13)

Go out into the world in peace; have courage; hold on to what is good; return no one evil for evil; strengthen the fainthearted; support the weak, and help the suffering; honor all people; love and serve the Lord, rejoicing in the power of the Holy Spirit.

(*Book of Common Worship*, p. 78)

As you depart this place and go into the world, remember to love the Lord your God with all your heart, with all your soul, with all your mind, and with all your strength; and to love your neighbor as yourself.

And whatever you do, in word or deed, do everything in the name of the Lord Jesus, giving thanks to God the Father through him.

(Col. 3:17)

Leader:	May God bless you and keep you.
People:	**Amen.**
Leader:	May God's face shine upon you and be gracious to you.
People:	**Amen.**
Leader:	May God look upon you with kindness and give you peace.
People:	**Amen.**
Leader:	Let us go forth into the world, rejoicing in the power of the Holy Spirit.
People:	**Thanks be to God!**

(*Book of Worship: United Church of Christ*, p. 75)

Leader:	We have worshiped God together;
People:	**Now we go our separate ways.**
Leader:	May the spirit which has blessed us here
People:	**Be your spirit in each day that comes! Amen.**

(*Book of Worship: United Church of Christ*, p. 553)

Then I heard the voice of the Lord saying, "Whom shall I send, and who will go for us?" And I said, "Here am I; send me!" And he said, "Go. . . ."

(Isa. 6:8-9*a*)

Leader:	We depart in faith.
People:	**Trusting God to guide us through this week.**
Leader:	We depart in hope.
People:	**Knowing God holds the future in God's hands.**
Leader:	We depart in love.
People:	**Serving others in the name of Christ.**
Leader:	We depart in faith, in hope, and in love.
People:	**Thanks be to God! Amen.**

Leader:	We are the church gathered,
People:	**now we become the church dispersed.**
Leader:	May the sustenance we have found here,
People:	**follow us wherever we go.**
Leader:	Through Jesus Christ our Lord,
People:	**Amen.**

118

Other examples of pastoral benedictions can be found in various denominational books of worship, or they can be written by the pastor or worship leader.

Closing Song

The closing song can be a traditional hymn or a contemporary song. Many churches observe a recessional during the closing song. The order for the recessional is the same as the processional (see chapter 2). Since the closing song sends the congregation into the world to serve God, it should usually be focused on mission and service. Examples of closing songs include

◇ "Let There Be Peace on Earth"
◇ "Freely, Freely"
◇ "Go, Tell It on the Mountain"
◇ "Lead On, O King Eternal"
◇ "Go Forth in His Name"
◇ "Jesu, Jesu, Fill Us with Your Love"
◇ "We've a Story to Tell to the Nations"
◇ "Go, Make of All Disciples"
◇ "Onward, Christian Soldiers"
◇ "God of Grace and God of Glory"
◇ "Whom Shall I Send?"
◇ "Here I Am, Lord"
◇ "The Trees of the Field"

On occasion sing a song of blessing, such as "God Be with You Till We Meet Again," "Grace to You," or "On Eagle's Wings," as the closing song. Another option is to have the choir sing a closing song of blessing or sending.

Words of Dismissal

For many churches, the closing song is the final act of worship, followed by instrumental music while the congregation leaves the place of worship. However, some churches add a final word of dismissal. After the closing song, the minister says (from the back of the church, if there has been a recessional), "Go in peace to love and serve the Lord." The congregation responds, "Thanks be to God." At that point, corporate worship comes to an end, and the service of God begins!

Chapter 7

An Example of Ancient~Modern Worship

P astor Stephens pulled into the church parking lot at 8:30 A.M. As he unlocked the front door of the sanctuary, he noticed Bill and Lucille's van parked near the side entrance. After opening the sanctuary doors, he walked to the kitchen where he found Bill and Lucille pouring Welch's grape juice into tiny Communion cups. Although Pastor Stephens lobbied for years to use a common cup for the Lord's Supper, he finally gave up the battle. Concern for germs won out over concern for symbolism. Still, the bigger battle had been won. First Church now celebrated weekly Communion, which made Pastor Stephens extremely happy.

After some small talk with Bill and Lucille, Pastor Stephens walked to his office. He looked again at the order of worship. He noticed that one of the hymn titles was misspelled. However, in spite of that minor detail, the worship bulletin looked fine. Pastor Stephens reviewed the service one final time. Under his leadership, First Church now ordered their worship services around five major movements:

> We Gather to Worship God
> We Listen to the Word of God
> We Respond to the Call of God
> We Celebrate at the Table of God
> We Depart to Serve God

As Pastor Stephens looked over his sermon notes, he glanced out his office window into the church parking lot. Numerous cars pulled up, and people began walking into the church. Pastor Stephens asked himself, as he had many times before, *What really brings these people to this place week after week?* It always amazed him to see people pull into the parking lot Sunday after Sunday and walk into the church.

Pastor Stephens glanced at his watch. Mable, director of the Adult III Sunday school department, had called earlier that morning. Her arthritis was acting up and she asked Pastor Stephens if he would preside at the opening assembly of her department. He happily agreed. Pastor Stephens loved the senior adults at First Church. They had been among his best supporters since beginning this pastorate four years earlier.

After leading the opening assembly for Mable, Pastor Stephens met with the lay worship leaders for the morning service. Final details were reviewed and the Lord's Table was put in order. Worship would begin shortly. Pastor Stephens left the sanctuary, put on his pulpit robe and stole, and met with several church leaders for a brief time of prayer.

We Gather to Worship God

At 10:30 A.M., Jane, the church organist, and Mark, a trumpet player, began the prelude. It was listed in the bulletin as "preparation for worship." As Jane and Mark played a rousing duet of "How Great Thou Art," nature slides from the Grand Canyon were projected onto a large screen. At the same time, Pastor Stephens, the choir, and other worship leaders gathered in the vestibule for the processional. The worship bulletin said, "We Gather to Worship God." Lynda, lay worship leader for the day, invited the congregation to stand for the call to worship—the same one the children used during last week's Vacation Bible School. Lynda began:

Leader:	The Lord be with you.
People:	**And also with you.**
Leader:	Who are you?
People:	**We are the people of God.**
Leader:	Who made you?
People:	**God, our Creator, made us.**
Leader:	Where do you live?
People:	**We live in God's good world.**
Leader:	Why are you here?
People:	**We are here to worship God.**
Leader:	Then let the worship begin!

(adapted from *Writing Your Own Worship Materials*, p. 23)

As the congregation began singing "All Creatures of Our God and King," the crossbearer, acolyte, banner carrier, choir, and Pastor Stephens processed down the center aisle. Upon reaching the platform, Pastor Stephens scouted out the congregation. *Not a bad crowd*, he thought. *It could be better, but it's not bad for summer*. After the hymn and opening prayer, Larry, a lay reader, led a responsive reading from Psalm 100. Two contemporary praise choruses followed. The second praise chorus included an interpretative liturgical dance by Jennifer, one of the members of the dance and drama team. Although numerous members disliked praise choruses, the young people loved them and lobbied strongly for their use. Like many churches, First Church struggled to meet the needs and wishes of a diverse congregation. After extensive discussion and numerous debates, the church decided that a blend of historic, traditional, and contemporary worship would work best for them. Although occasional skirmishes still continued, this compromise seemed to work fairly well.

During the choruses, Pastor Stephens looked carefully at the congregation. Near the front of the sanctuary, on the right side, sat Donna. Donna recently received a major promotion at First Citizens' bank. Near the back, with the other teenagers, sat David. Last week David received a large scholarship at a prestigious university. Jeff and Gerri sat on the left, near the front. They just discovered Gerri was pregnant, and they seemed to glow with joy. On the back left pew, all alone, sat Mary. Her divorce was finalized last Friday. On the front row, as always, sat Marvin and his wife, Jewell. Marvin was diagnosed with bone cancer a few months earlier, and his prognosis was bleak. Near the middle of the church, on the left side, sat Thelma. Although eight months had passed since Thelma's husband died, she still struggled deeply with grief. In one of the middle pews on the right side sat Charles, looking tired and strained. Pastor Stephens visited Charles a few days earlier. Charles, one of First Church's best members, was a deeply committed Christian. Unfortunately, the weak economy finally took its toll and Charles lost his business. "It's not fair," Charles protested during his visit with Pastor Stephens. "I've worked hard. I've treated my employees well. I've tried to be a good Christian. I've prayed for God's help, but nothing has happened. I feel like God has abandoned me." Pastor Stephens glanced at Charles several times during the opening songs of the gathering. Charles was not singing.

We Listen to the Word of God

The worship bulletin now said, "We Listen to the Word of God." Over the past year, the worship council at First Church worked hard to add variety to the weekly Scripture readings. For example, the drama team often performed brief drama sketches that related to the day's text and sermon. Since today's Gospel lesson involved dialogue between biblical characters, the worship council enlisted several people to read the passage in a dialogue style. Keith read the words of Jesus, Bill read the words of Peter, and Pat served as narrator, reading all the nondialogue parts. This dialogical approach, which First Church often used with appropriate texts, seemed to help Scripture come alive for the congregation. At the conclusion of the Scripture reading, Pat said, "This is the word of God for the people of God." The congregation enthusiastically responded, "Thanks be to God!" At that point, the choir sang a peppy new arrangement of an old hymn, complete with synthesizer, trumpet, and drums. The congregation joined in on the final stanza. Pastor Stephens stood to preach his sermon. His introduction included a brief video clip from a popular movie. After the media presentation, Pastor Stephens continued his sermon, using a narrative, "storytelling" style of communication.

We Respond to the Call of God

The worship bulletin now said, "We Respond to the Call of God." First Church usually provided four opportunities for congregational response. They were listed in the worship bulletin as *God's Call to Faith, God's Call to Prayer, God's Call to Stewardship,* and *God's Call to Community* (the passing of the peace).

After the invitation to discipleship, and a hymn of response, Pastor Stephens led the congregation in reciting the Apostles' Creed. Although they often recited the Apostles' or Nicene Creed, First Church also used other affirmations of faith, both ancient and contemporary. During the creed, Pastor Stephens glanced again at Charles, the businessman who felt abandoned by God. He saw Charles saying, "I believe in God the Father Almighty, maker of heaven and earth; and in Jesus Christ his only Son our Lord. . . ."

A time of congregational prayer was next, followed by the offering. Pastor Stephens hoped today's offering would be a good one. They were behind budget, and the finance committee was getting nervous. After the offering, the congregation stood to sing the doxology. Finally, the congregation shared in the passing of the peace. Pastor Stephens said to the congregation, "The peace of Christ be with you." The congregation responded, "And also with you." At that point people shook hands, hugged, and greeted one another throughout the sanctuary. Although some members resisted it at first, the passing of the peace soon became a vibrant time of love, fellowship, and community at First Church. Visitors seemed especially impressed by the warmth generated during this special time of worship. The passing of the peace ended with the singing of the chorus "Surely the Presence of the Lord."

We Celebrate at the Table of God

The bulletin now said, "We Celebrate at the Table of God." Pastor Stephens stood directly behind the Lord's Supper table. As the elements were brought forward and placed on the table, the congregation sang a contemporary chorus: "Open our eyes, Lord; we want to see Jesus. . . ." Then Pastor Stephens and the congregation spoke the ancient opening words from the Great Thanksgiving:

Leader:	The Lord be with you.
People:	**And also with you.**
Leader:	Lift up your hearts.
People:	**We lift them up to the Lord.**
Leader:	Let us give thanks to the Lord our God.
People:	**It is right to give our thanks and praise.**

Pastor Stephens continued:

It is right, and a good and joyful thing, always and everywhere to give thanks to you, Father Almighty, creator of heaven and earth. . . . And so, with your people on earth and all the company of heaven we praise your name and join their unending hymn.

At that point the instruments began to play and the congregation began to sing the ancient, holy words:

Holy, holy, holy Lord, God of power and might, heaven and earth are full of your glory. Hosanna in the highest. Blessed is he who comes in the name of the Lord. Hosanna in the highest.

Pastor Stephens continued the Great Thanksgiving prayer, as priests and ministers have done for almost two thousand years in preparation for Communion. As he led the prayer, Pastor Stephens felt deep gratitude for the privilege of leading Eucharist.

After the Great Thanksgiving, the Lord's Prayer, and breaking of the bread, Pastor Stephens held up the elements and said, "These are the gifts of God for the people of God. Let us partake with glad and generous hearts." He then invited the congregation to come forward to receive Communion. For those who wanted it, an opportunity was also given to receive prayer, anointing with oil, and laying on of hands.

At that point, several lay ministers came to the table to assist in the distribution of the elements. As the congregation sang celebrative hymns and choruses, and as people made their way to the Lord's Table, Pastor Stephens asked himself again, *Why do these people return to this place week after week? Why do they get up, get dressed, fuss with kids, get into the car, drive to the parking lot, and enter this sanctuary?*

As he handed out wafers of bread and said, "The body of Christ, given for you," Pastor Stephens knew why they came. It was not just habit, or feelings of obligation, or guilt. No, it went deeper than that. Pastor Stephens knew one reason they came was because they needed one another. It is a hard world and people need comrades to survive. But something even more profound than human connection kept them coming. Ultimately, they came to this place because they needed God. They came because they needed to acknowledge that One exists who is greater than themselves. They came to encounter the living Lord, and to be reminded in tangible and concrete ways that they belong to God and that God loved them. Somehow, through that worship, they found the strength to carry on another week. And somehow, through that worship, First Church also found the strength to carry on another week.

We Depart to Serve God

By now all had received the bread and cup of Communion. The worship bulletin said, "We Depart to Serve God." The congregation stood and prayed together:

> Eternal God, we give you thanks for this holy mystery in which you have given yourself to us. Grant that we may go into the world in the strength of your Spirit, to give ourselves for others, in the name of Jesus Christ our Lord. Amen.

Pastor Stephens then lifted his right hand and said to the congregation, "Go now to love and serve the Lord. And as you go, may the grace of the Lord Jesus Christ, the love of God, and the communion of the Holy Spirit be with all of you." The congregation then sang a closing song of commitment; the choir and worship leaders recessed out; and the service concluded.

Pastor Stephens stood at the back of the church greeting people while the ushers straightened up the sanctuary. Finally, everyone was gone. Pastor Stephens stood alone in the sanctuary. As usual, he walked to the pulpit to pick up his Bible and sermon notes. But today, for some reason, he paused a moment and looked at the empty sanctuary. And as he looked he remembered something he had not thought about in a long time. He remembered a story he had heard told years earlier.

The story goes like this: On Monday morning, a custodian arrived at a church to clean and sweep up the sanctuary. However, this week he did not find the usual fare—forgotten Bibles, umbrellas, bulletins covered with children's scribbling, and torn-up notes that teenagers wrote during Sunday's service. No, this week the custodian found very different items indeed.

On a middle pew on the right side of the church laid a discouraged man's anger toward God. On the back left pew sat a woman's profound disappointment and her fear of an unknown future. Further down the pew laid a middle-aged father's feelings of failure. Across the aisle the custodian found a young couple's lukewarm commitment. On the front row he discovered an old man's fear of death. In the corner, so small that one could barely see it, laid a young person's sins. On other pews he found bitterness, pride, jealousy, fear, and doubt. It was like this all over the sanctuary. The custodian was not sure what to do. Finally, he swept it all up—all the wounds and hurts and fears and sins—and he threw them away.

Still thinking about the story, Pastor Stephens took one more look at the empty sanctuary. As he walked outside to the parking lot he said to himself, "This is what it's all about. This is what it's really all about."

Appendix 1

Sample Orders of Worship

The following order of worship comes from a series of worship services based on the Lord's Prayer. This particular worship service was based on the phrase "hallowed be thy name."

We Gather to Worship God

Welcome and Announcements
Preparation for Worship: "As the Deer"
 (Solo accompanied by sign language)
Call to Worship:

Leader:	Blessed be God: Father, Son, and Holy Spirit.
People:	**And blessed be God's kingdom, now and forever.**
Leader:	Lord, open our lips,
People:	**and our mouths shall proclaim your praise.**

Processional Hymn: "All Creatures of Our God and King"
Opening Prayer:

Almighty God, to you all hearts are open, all desires known, and from you no secrets are hid: Cleanse the thoughts of our hearts by the inspiration of your Holy

Spirit, that we may perfectly love you, and worthily magnify your holy Name; through Christ our Lord. Amen.

(Book of Common Prayer, p. 355)

Responsive Reading of Psalm 100
Songs of Praise: "Great Is the Lord" and "Glorify Thy Name"

We Listen to the Word of God

Drama Sketch: *God of the Bumper Stickers*
Choral Reading of Revelation 4:8-11 and 5:11-14
Choir Anthem: "Worthy of Worship"
  (Congregation joins in on third stanza)
Sermon: "Hallowed Be Thy Name"

We Respond to the Call of God

God's Call to Faith
  Song of Response: "Majesty, Worship His Majesty"
  Affirmation of Faith: The Nicene Creed
God's Call to Prayer
  Sharing of Joys and Concerns
  Prayers of the People
God's Call to Stewardship
  Offering
  The Doxology
God's Call to Community
  The Passing of the Peace
  Chorus: "I Love You, Lord"

We Celebrate at the Table of God

Invitation to the Sacrament of Holy Communion
Communion Chorus: "Open Our Eyes, Lord"
The Great Thanksgiving
The Lord's Prayer
The Sacrament of Holy Communion
Communion Songs: "Surely the Presence," "Holy, Holy, Holy," "Sing Hallelujah to the Lord," "Fairest Lord Jesus"

We Depart to Serve God

Closing Prayer:

Eternal God, we give you thanks for this holy mystery in which you have given yourself to us. Grant that we may go into the world in the strength of your Spirit, to give ourselves for others, in the name of Jesus Christ our Lord. Amen.

Pastoral Benediction
Recessional Hymn: "Here I Am, Lord"
Words of Dismissal:

Sometimes seasonal or special services will determine the need for a different worship outline. The following are worship outlines that have been used for the Christmas season, the season of Lent, and Pentecost Sunday. Although the wording differs slightly, each follows the historic fivefold movement of worship.

Christmas Season
(from Luke 2:8-20)

They Saw God's Glory

"In that region there were shepherds . . . keeping watch over their flock by night. Then an angel of the Lord stood before them, and the glory of the Lord shone around them. . . ."

Welcome and Announcements
Preparation for Worship
Call to Worship
Processional Hymn
Opening Prayer
Songs of Praise

They Heard God's Word

"The angel said to them, 'Do not be afraid; for see—I am bringing you good news of great joy for all the people."

131

Prayer for Illumination
Dialogue Scripture Reading
Congregational Hymn
Dramatic Monologue Sermon

They Responded to God's Word

"The shepherds said to one another, 'Let us go now to Bethlehem and see this thing that has taken place' . . . So they went with haste. . . ."

God's Call to Faith
    Song of Response
    Affirmation of Faith
God's Call to Prayer
    Invitation to Prayer
    Prayers of the People
God's Call to Stewardship
    Offering
    The Doxology
God's Call to Community
    The Passing of the Peace
    Chorus

They Were Given a Sign

"This will be a sign for you; you will find a child wrapped in bands of cloth and lying in a manger."

Invitation to Holy Communion
Communion Chorus
The Great Thanksgiving
The Lord's Prayer
The Sacrament of Holy Communion
Communion Songs

They Went Home Renewed

"The shepherds returned [home], glorifying and praising God for all they had heard and seen, as it had been told them."

Closing Prayer
Pastoral Benediction
Recessional Hymn
Words of Dismissal

Season of Lent
(from Luke 22:14-23, 39)

They Gathered with Jesus

"When the hour came [for the Passover Meal], Jesus took his place at the table, and the apostles with him."

They Listened to Jesus

"Jesus said to them, 'I have eagerly desired to eat this Passover with you before I suffer, for I tell you. . . .' "

They Responded to Jesus

"Then they began to ask one another, which one of them it could be. . . ."

They Communed with Jesus

"Then he took a loaf of bread, and when he had given thanks, he broke it and gave it to them, saying, 'This is my body, which is given for you. Do this in remembrance of me.' And he did the same with the cup after supper, saying, 'This cup that is poured out for you is the new covenant in my blood.' "

133

They Departed, Following Jesus

"He came out and went, as was his custom, to the Mount of Olives; and the disciples followed him."

Pentecost Sunday
(Acts 2)

They Gathered and Were Filled with the Spirit

"When the day of Pentecost had come, they were all together in one place. . . . All of them were filled with the Holy Spirit. . . ."

They Listened to God's Word

"But Peter, standing with the eleven, raised his voice and addressed them . . . 'listen to what I say.' "

They Responded to God's Word

"Now when they heard this, they were cut to the heart and said to Peter and to the other apostles, 'Brothers, what should we do?' "

They Broke Bread Together

"They devoted themselves to . . . the breaking of bread. . . ."

They Served God in Their Community

"Many wonders and signs were being done . . . ; they would sell their possessions and goods and distribute the proceeds. . . ."

Appendix 2

Resource Listing

General Resources

Brown, Paul B. *In and for the World: Bringing the Contemporary into Christian Worship* (Minneapolis: Fortress Press, 1992). How to connect worship to what is happening in the world, with numerous examples and an extensive list of worship resources.

Crouch, Timothy J. *And Also with You: Worship Resources Based on the Revised Common Lectionary: Years A, B, and C* (Akron, Ohio: The Order of St. Luke of The United Methodist Church, 1992, 1993, and 1994). Each contains an opening prayer for every Sunday of the year, a call to worship, a general prayer for the day, hymn suggestions, and artwork for bulletin front covers. To order this resource, call (800) 672-1789.

Dawn, Marva J. *Reaching Out Without Dumbing Down: A Theology of Worship for the Turn-of-the-Century Culture* (Grand Rapids: Eerdmans, 1995). A provocative critique of contemporary worship.

Duck, Ruth, ed. *Bread for the Journey: Resources for Worship* (Cleveland: Pilgrim Press, 1981). Practical worship aids.

Haymes, Peggy A. *Be Thou Present: Prayer, Litanies, and Hymns for Christian Worship* (Macon, Ga.: Smyth & Helwys Publishing, 1994). Useful prayers and litanies.

Hock, Mary Isabelle. *Worship Through the Seasons: Ideas for Celebration* (San Jose, Calif.: Resource Publications, 1987).

Schaffran, Janet, and Pat Kozak. *More Than Words: Prayer and Ritual for Inclusive Communities* (New York: The Crossroad, 1986).

Sparkman, G. Temp. *Writing Your Own Worship Materials* (Valley Forge, Pa.: Judson Press, 1980).

Thurian, Max, and Geoffrey Wainwright, eds. *Baptism and Eucharist: Ecumenical Convergence in Celebration* (Grand Rapids: Eerdmans, 1983).

Webber, Robert, ed. *The Complete Library of Christian Worship* (Peabody, Mass.: Hendrickson Publishers, 1994). The seven large volumes of this remarkable and comprehensive worship encyclopedia include such subjects as biblical and historical foundations of worship, worship renewal, music and the arts in worship, the church year, and the sacraments. Full of practical examples. Highly recommended.

Webber is one of the leading authorities in worship today. His books are well written and include valuable insights into the worship of God. Webber's works include *Worship: Old and New*. 2d ed. (Grand Rapids: Zondervan, 1994); *Worship Is a Verb!* (Nashville: Star Song Publishing Group, 1992); *Blended Worship: Achieving Substance and Relevance in Worship* (Peabody, Mass.: Hendrickson Publishers, 1996); and *Planning Blended Worship: The Creative Mixture of Old and New* (Nashville: Abingdon Press, 1998).

White, James. *Introduction to Christian Worship*. 2d. ed. (Nashville: Abingdon Press, 1990). An excellent introduction to worship. Highly recommended.

Denominational Books of Worship

Among the most helpful worship resources are denominational books of worship. Examples include:

Christian Church (Disciples of Christ): *Thankful Praise: A Resource for Christian Worship* (St. Louis: CBP Press, 1987).

Episcopal: *The Book of Common Prayer* (The Church Hymnal Corporation and the Seabury Press, 1979). Highly recommended.

Lutheran: *Lutheran Book of Worship: Ministers Desk Edition* (Minneapolis: Augsburg Publishing House, 1978).

Presbyterian: *Book of Common Worship* (Louisville: Westminster/John Knox Press, 1993). Highly recommended.

United Church of Christ: *Book of Worship: United Church of Christ* (New York: United Church of Christ Office for Church Life and Leadership, 1986).

The United Methodist: *The United Methodist Book of Worship* (Nashville: The United Methodist Publishing House, 1992). Highly recommended.

Specific Topics

Banners

Harms, Carol Jean. *Banners for Worship* (St. Louis: Concordia, 1990). A good resource for a beginning banner ministry.

Webber, *The Complete Library of Christian Worship*. See vol. 4, "Music and the Arts in Christian Worship."

Bulletin Artwork

ClickArt: Christian Graphics. Broderbund Software Inc., Novato, Calif. These two CD-ROMs contain thousands of Christian graphics, many of which are appropriate for the front cover of worship bulletins. Order from a computer software supplier.

Church Year

Hickman, Hoyt, ed. *The New Handbook of the Christian Year* (Nashville: Abingdon Press, 1992). An excellent overview of the seasons of the Christian year, with complete orders of worship. If you only purchase one book on this subject, this should be the one.

Stookey, Laurence Hull. *Calendar: Christ's Time for the Church* (Nashville: Abingdon Press, 1966). A good introduction to the Christian calendar.

Congregational Singing

Traditional hymn collections can be found in any denominational hymnbook.

Contemporary song collections can be ordered from Brentwood Benson Music Company in Nashville, Tennessee, including *America's 25 Praise and Worship*, vols. 1 and 2; *America's 200 Favorite Choruses and Hymns*; and *Lift Him Up*, vols. 1 through 5. To order a catalog of these and other Brentwood Benson Music resources, call (800) 546-2539.

Blended collections, containing both traditional hymns and contemporary songs, are also available. They include *Renew! Songs and Hymns for Blended Worship* (Carol Stream, Ill.: Hope Publishing, 1995); and *Celebration Hymnal: Songs and Hymns for Worship* (Word Music/Integrity Music, 1997). Highly recommended.

Dance

Hock, Mary Isabelle. *Worship Through the Seasons.* Creative worship ideas, including liturgical movement and dance. To order this book, call (888) 273-7782.

Webber, *The Complete Library of Christian Worship.* See vol. 4, book 2, "Music and the Arts in Christian Worship," pp. 719-769. In this section is a historical background of liturgical dance, a rationale for using dance, numerous examples, and a helpful bibliography that lists numerous liturgical dance resources.

Drama

Perry, Michael, ed. *The Dramatized Old Testament* and *The Dramatized New Testament* (Grand Rapids, Mich.: Baker Book House, 1996 [OT] and 1993 [NT]). Excellent resources that have arranged, in script format, passages from throughout the Bible.

Webber, *The Complete Library of Christian Worship*. See vol. 4, "Music and the Arts in Christian Worship," for an excellent section on drama, including numerous examples.

Welton, John Lee. *Drama for All Occasions* (Nashville: Convention Press, 1991). Good collection of one-act plays, brief stretches, monologues, and reader's theater readings.

Most denominational publishing houses now carry drama resources, including my own denomination, The United Methodist Church. Call (800) 672-1789 for a catalog.

Most Christian bookstores carry at least a few drama resources:

CSS Publishing offers a good selection of drama resources, especially for special seasons of the year. The publications include plays, pageants, reader's theater, and monologues. The company also has a good selection of worship and preaching resources. Call (800) 537-1030 for a catalog.

Resource Publications Inc., out of San Jose, California, has several good drama resources, including *Three-Minute Dramas for Worship* by Karen Patitucci (1989). The company also carries several excellent storytelling and banner resources. For a catalog, call (888) 273-7782.

Willow Creek Community Church in South Barrington, Illinois, is well known for its use of short dramatic sketches in worship. These sketches can be used as a powerful introduction to a worship or sermon theme. To obtain a free copy of the drama sketches catalog, call (800) 876-7335. Also available are the "Sunday Morning Live" drama packages, which include a script and videotape of six different drama sketches.

Perhaps the most impressive resource for Christian drama is Lillenas Drama Resources out of Kansas City, Missouri. Lillenas has extensive drama resources, including books on how to begin a drama ministry, full-length plays, reader's theater products, dramas for special occasions, and a huge selection of drama sketches. For a free catalog of Lillenas products, call (800) 877-0700.

For a comprehensive listing of more than five hundred production resources, from drama scripts to costumes, lighting, props, and even wigs and beards, call Production Resources at (503) 977-2923 and ask about *The Resource Book*. It currently lists for $34.95. A brochure explaining *The Resource Book* is available at no cost.

Sacraments

Denominational books of worship (see above) provide helpful guidance on celebrating the sacraments, including full liturgies for Communion, baptism, and reaffirmation of baptism vows.

O'Donnell, Michael. *Lift Up Your Hearts*, rev. ed. (Akron, Ohio: OSL Publications, 1994). Lectionary-based Great Thanksgiving prayers for each Sunday of the year. Order at (800) 672-1789.

Stookey, Laurence Hull. *Eucharist: Christ's Feast with the Church* (Nashville: Abingdon Press, 1993). Good overview of the Sacrament of Holy Communion.

Webber, *The Complete Library of Christian Worship*. See vol. 6, "The Sacred Actions of Christian Worship."

White, James. *Sacraments as God's Self Giving* (Nashville: Abingdon Press, 1983). Excellent introduction to the sacraments.

Slides from Jesus of Nazareth

Information about slides from the movie *Jesus of Nazareth*, mentioned in chapter 3, can be received from Phil Barfoot Music Company, Brentwood Benson Music Publishing Company, 365 Great Circle Road, Nashville, TN 37228. For a catalog, call (800) 546-2539.

Using Copyrighted Materials

Information on seeking permission for the use of copyrighted materials for worship services can be obtained from the following sources:

Christian Copyright Licensing International offers permission for songs to help congregations comply with copyright laws. For more information, contact

CCLI
17201 NE Sacramento Street
Portland, OR 97230
(800) 234-2446
www.ccli.com

The Motion Picture Licensing Corporation, authorized by major motion picture studios and independent producers, grants licenses to nonprofit organizations for the public performances of videocassettes and videodiscs. For more information, contact

MPLC
5455 Centinela Ave.
Los Angeles, CA 90066-6970
(800) 462-8855
www.mplc.com

For general information about copyright laws, contact

U.S. Copyright Office
Library of Congress
101 Independence Ave. SE
Washington, D.C. 20559-6000
www.loc.gov/copyright/